ACKNOWLEDGMENTS

Much love to . . .

Kristen for stepping up to the whiteboard

Jon for taking a crack at an early draft

Don for Monday lunches in remote caves

Marsha for meeting us at Kava House

Tomaas for giving me seven of the best numbers in the world

Tandy for focus, focus, focus

Matt Krick for the keen mind and giant heart

René for believing more than ever

Kathy for wisdom, perspective, and the details

The Mars Hill Tribe for going there again and again

Chris for making Grand Rapids your second home

Angela for another joyous round

Sister Virginia for showing me that there's never been anything to prove

SEX
GOD

EXPLORING THE ENDLESS QUESTIONS BETWEEN SPIRITUALITY AND SEXUALITY

ROB BELL

Published in 2012 by Collins

HarperCollins*Publishers*
77–85 Fulham Palace Road
London W6 8JB

www.harpercollins.co.uk

First published by Zondervan in 2007
This edition 2012

10 9 8 7 6 5 4 3 2 1

A catalogue record for this book is available from the British Library.

ISBN: 978-0-00-748785-1

Printed and bound in Great Britain by Clays Ltd, St Ives plc.

CONTENTS

THIS IS REALLY ABOUT THAT

Once there were two brothers.

Jacob had smooth skin. But his older brother, Esau, was "a hairy man."

And not only was Esau follicly well-endowed, he loved to be outdoors. He was a skillful hunter—picture Ted Nugent in sandals. His smooth-skinned brother? Jacob stayed inside and cooked and hung out with their mother.

You can smell the conflict coming.

Which it does. Their father, Isaac, was dying, and the custom in the ancient Near East at that time was for the father to give his blessing to his firstborn son before he passed away. This was a symbolic gesture loaded with significance. Isaac sends Esau out to kill an animal they can eat as part of the blessing ceremony. But Jacob, at his mother's prodding, covers himself in goat skins and goes to his ailing blind father, pretending to be Esau.

When Isaac hears him, he asks who it is, and Jacob responds, "I am Esau your firstborn."[1]

Jacob insists he's someone else.

Isaac falls for the deception and gives Jacob the blessing he intended to give Esau. Jacob's lie is a serious offense against the family, against Isaac, and ultimately against Esau. And when Esau finds out, he's furious and makes it clear that when their father dies, he is going to kill Jacob.

Which Jacob takes as a subtle hint that it's time to leave town.

So Jacob is on the move, running for his life, when he stops to sleep for the night. The Bible describes the spot where he rests as "a certain place."[2] This detail is significant because this is not a religious site; it isn't the top of a mountain or the edge of the sea, there isn't a temple nearby. Jacob falls asleep in a random place by the side of the road. That night, he has a dream. An intense dream in which God speaks to him and says, among other things, "I am with you and will watch over you wherever you go, and I will bring you back to this land. I will not leave you until I have done what I have promised you."[3]

What God does here is astounding. People at that time believed the gods resided in religious places, places where gods are expected to be—temples and holy sites and shrines and altars.[4] But this God is different.

This God appears at rest areas.
This God speaks to people at "certain places" along
the way.
This God doesn't need temples and holy sites and rituals.
This God will speak to anybody, anywhere, anytime.

Jacob then takes a stone and sets it up as a pillar to mark
the spot, making a vow: "If God will be with me and will
watch over me on this journey I am taking and will give
me food to eat and clothes to wear so that I return safely
to my father's household, then the Lord will be my God."[5]

Years pass. Jacob marries, starts a family, and eventually
reconciles with Esau. He stops pretending to be someone
he's not. And then one day he returns to the spot where
he made his vow to God. The book of Genesis says, "He
built an altar, and he called the place El Bethel, because it
was there that God revealed himself to him when he was
fleeing from his brother."[6]

Bet is the Hebrew word for house. *El* is one of the names
for God. Bethel, the "House of God."

Imagine you're one of Jacob's kids: you have just arrived
in this new land, and there's a stone pillar there that your
dad can't stop talking about. He's telling anyone who will
listen this story about something that happened to him
years ago, and he's stacking rocks on top of rocks. He's
stacking them so high, he turns the whole thing into an
altar. And he keeps talking about a vow he made to God,
and you have no idea what the point of this is. It seems a

bit much. And then he starts calling this pile of rocks the House of God.

What if you asked, "Dad, what's the big deal? They're just rocks."[7]

I imagine Jacob would respond, "Yes, you're right, they're rocks, but they're more than rocks. You have to understand, I was on the run and thought my brother was going to kill me. My life was over. And God saved me. And God brought me to a new home. And I had food to eat and a place to sleep and eventually God gave me a family. These aren't just rocks. These are a symbol of life for me. God came through for me."

They're rocks, but they're more than rocks.

We do this all the time.

If we were to go through your garage or storage shelves or sock drawer, I guarantee we would find the strangest things. I have a trophy from when I was fourteen. The little man on the top fell off sometime in the '90s, the lettering that says what it's for has faded, and the years have revealed that, shockingly, that isn't real marble. But I've kept it. I haven't thrown it away because it's more than a trophy to me. That trophy is the first time I actually won something on my own. It represents a certain period of my life and the struggles of being fourteen and finding my identity and wondering if I'd ever be good at anything.

It's a trophy, but it's more than a trophy.

Jewelry, pictures, sculptures made by children, antiques that have been in the family for years, art projects, souvenirs, velvet paintings—we hold on to them because they point beyond themselves. If we were to ask you about a certain picture and why you have it displayed in such a prominent place in your home or office or why you carry it in your purse or wallet everywhere you go, you'd probably respond by talking about the people in the picture, where it was taken, when it was taken. But that would only be the start. Those relationships and that place and that time are all about something else, something more. If we kept exploring, you'd probably end up using words like trust and love and belonging and commitment and celebration.

So it's a picture, but it's more than a picture.

This physical thing—this picture, trophy, artifact, gift—is actually about that relationship, that truth, that reality, that moment in time.

This is actually about *that.*

Whether it's what we do with our energies
or how we feel about our bodies
or wanting to have the control in relationships
or trying to recover from heartbreak
or dealing with our ferocious appetites
or the difficulty of communicating clearly with those
we love

or longing for something or someone better,
much of life is in some way connected with our sexuality.

And when we begin to sort through all of the issues
surrounding our sexuality, we quickly end up in the
spiritual,

because this
is always about that.

And so this guy always has a girlfriend, and it has
become a joke among his family and friends that the day
he loses one girlfriend, he finds another—they actually
use the phrase "trade her in" behind his back—which
raises the question, Why does he need to have a girl?
What is his real need, the one that drives him to need a
girl? And if we could get at that, would he not need a girl
so much?

And she's got a coldness in her heart toward her
husband, but it's really about something that happened
years before she even met him.

And he's got this thing he does, and he keeps telling her
that all guys are like this, and she wants to trust him, but
she's dying to know if all guys really are like him, because
it's getting a little weird.

And she's single and fine with it but still has this sense
that she's a sexual being, and she's trying to figure out
how to reconcile this because her married friends
keep trying to set her up with a "nice" guy they know,

which gives her the feeling that her friends think she is somehow incomplete because she isn't married.

And they keep having these arguments about things that are so trivial it's embarrassing. Yesterday they got into it over how the cars should be parked, and the day before it had something to do with the phone bill, and before that it was about whose turn it was to take the dog out, and now it's happening again—they're in the kitchen debating how a tomato should be properly sliced. They've been living together now for several years, and they would say it's been great, but they're at this point in the relationship where issues like trust and commitment and future and kids and marriage are starting to linger in their minds and hearts, and underneath it all they both have this question: Are you the one? But neither of them has ever actually voiced it, and both of them experienced their parents' divorcing at a young age, so anytime the subject of marriage comes up, things get confusing and tense very quickly, and so they're just at this moment realizing that this argument really has nothing to do with how to slice a tomato.

Because this is really about that.
It's always about something else.

Something deeper. Something behind it all. You can't talk about sexuality without talking about how we were made. And that will inevitably lead you to who made us. At some point you have to talk about God.

Sex. God. They're connected. And they can't be separated. Where the one is, you will always find the other. This is a book about how sexuality is the "this" and spirituality is the "that." To make sense of the one, we have to explore the other.

And *that* is what *this* book is about.

CHAPTER ONE

GOD WEARS LIPSTICK

In 1945, a group of British soldiers liberated a German concentration camp called Bergen-Belsen. One of them, Lieutenant Colonel Mercin Willet Gonin DSO, wrote in his diary about what they encountered:

> I can give no adequate description of the Horror Camp in which my men and myself were to spend the next month of our lives. It was just a barren wilderness, as bare as a chicken run. Corpses lay everywhere, some in huge piles, sometimes they lay singly or in pairs where they had fallen. It took a little time to get used to seeing men, women and children collapse as you walked by them. . . . One knew that five hundred a day were dying and that five hundred a day were going on dying for weeks before anything we could do would have the slightest effect. It was, however, not easy to watch a child choking to death from diphtheria when you knew a tracheotomy and nursing would save it. One

saw women drowning in their own vomit because they were too weak to turn over, men eating worms as they clutched a half loaf of bread purely because they had to eat worms to live and now could scarcely tell the difference. Piles of corpses, naked and obscene, with a woman too weak to stand propping herself against them as she cooked the food we had given her over an open fire; men and women crouching down just anywhere in the open relieving themselves . . . [a] dysentery tank in which the remains of a child floated.[1]

This account is shocking, horrible, and tragic. But why?
Because people shouldn't eat worms?
Because people shouldn't make piles of corpses?

We answer yes to these questions because no one should be forced to live in conditions such as those at Bergen-Belsen. And yet we intuitively understand that the wrong being done to these prisoners—these *people*—was much more significant than just the physical conditions forced upon them. A concentration camp is designed to strip people of their humanity.

It's anti-human.

And in the scriptures, anything that's anti-human is anti-God. Genesis begins with God creating the world and then creating people "in his own image."[2] The Hebrew word for *image* here is *tselem*, and it has a specific cultural meaning.[3] The stories of Genesis originated in ancient Near Eastern culture, where a king was said to rule in the image of a particular god. The famous King Tut is an Egyptian example of this. His full name was Tutankhamen, which is translated "the living image of [the god] Amon." The king was seen as the embodiment of a particular god on earth. If you wanted to see what that god was like, you looked at that god's king.

The writer of Genesis makes it clear that in all of creation there is something different about humans.[4] They aren't God, and they aren't going to become God, but in some distinct, intentional way, something of God has been placed in them. We reflect what God is like and who God is. A divine spark resides in every single human being.[5]

Everybody, everywhere. Bearers of the divine image.[6]

Picture a group of high school boys standing by their lockers when a girl walks by. One of the boys asks, "How do you rate that?" They then take turns assigning numerical values to the various parts of her anatomy, discussing in great detail how they evaluate her physical attributes.[7]

This scenario happens all the time, all over the world, every day. It's a pastime for some. There are television shows and websites and endless discussions all devoted to deciding who's hot and who's not. It's an industry, a form of entertainment, a culture.

And it's everywhere.

The problem is that "that" is actually a "she." A person. A woman. With a name, a history, with feelings. It seems harmless until you're that girl—and then it hurts. It's degrading. It's violating. It does something to a person's soul.

When a "She" Becomes a "That"

Jesus had much to say about what happens when a woman, an image-bearer, a carrier of the divine spark, becomes a "that." In the book of Matthew, Jesus teaches that "anyone who looks at a woman lustfully has already committed adultery with her in his heart."[8] He connects our eyes and our intentions and our thoughts with the state of our hearts.[9]

Jesus then takes it farther. He says, "If your right eye causes you to stumble, gouge it out and throw it away."

Which is a bit violent. Not to mention painful. And if taken literally, renders half of the human race blind in a matter of moments. Not to mention that blind people are fully capable of lusting. Our only conclusion is that Jesus is using the "it's merely a flesh wound" picture here to point us to something else.[10] Some truth beyond the removing of body parts. If we're not supposed to take it literally, then how, or where, are we supposed to take it?

Jesus explains by saying, "It is better for you to lose one part of your body than for your whole body to go into hell."

How did we get from lust, which is so common and doesn't seem like that big of a deal, to having your body thrown into hell in just a couple of sentences?

And to avoid this fate you should cut off your hand? Poke out your eye? *That* would be better?

He's stretching it a bit, isn't he?
Or did we miss something?

To understand how Jesus makes these connections, we have to explore the first-century Jewish understanding of heaven.

In the book of Psalms, it's written: "The Lord has established his throne in heaven, and his kingdom rules over all."[11] To the Jewish mind, heaven is not a fixed, unchanging geographical location somewhere other than this world. Heaven is the realm where things are as God intends them to be. The place where things are under the rule and reign of God. And that place can be anywhere, anytime, with anybody.

It's also written in the Psalms that "the highest heavens belong to the Lord, but the earth he has given to humankind."[12] So there is this realm, heaven, where things are as God wants them, under the rule and reign of God. But the earth is different. God has allowed for the temporary existence of other kingdoms. Other realms of authority. The earth "he has given to humankind." Which means we can do whatever we want. We can live however we want. We can choose to live under the rule and reign of God, or we can choose to rebel against God and live some other way.

Now if there's a realm where things are as God wants them to be, then there must be a realm where things are not as God wants them to be. Where things aren't according to God's will. Where people aren't treated as fully human.

It's called hell.

Think about the expression "for the hell of it." When someone says "for the hell of it," what they mean is that whatever is being discussed was done or said for no apparent reason. It was, in essence, pointless. Random. And God is *for* purpose and beauty and meaning.

When we say something was a "living hell," we mean that it was void of any love or peace or beauty or meaning. It was absent of the will and desire of God.

We hear about war zones being like hell, working conditions being hellish, a divorce being emotional hell, a famine feeling like hell on earth.[13]

Concentration camps are hells on earth.

And that's Jesus's point with the "gouge out your eye" teaching. His point isn't that you should mutilate your body if you find yourself lusting after someone. His point is that something serious—sometimes hellish—happens when people are treated as objects, and we should resist it at all costs.[14]

Right Now

When Jesus talks about heaven and hell, they are first and foremost present realities that have serious implications for the future. Either can be invited to earth, right now, through our actions.

It's possible for heaven to invade earth.
And it's possible for hell to invade earth.

A friend of mine talks honestly about how he spent years exploiting women for sex. He knew exactly what to say, how to act. He was a master at finding a woman who had a troubled relationship with her father and manipulating the situation for his pleasure. The first time he was telling me his story, he made a profound point that is true for all of us. He said that exploiting women for sex didn't just rob them of their humanity, it robbed him of his as well. As the years went on, he found that he didn't like what was happening to him. He was becoming less human in the process.

He said he was becoming a monster.

In treating women as objects, he was losing something of his own humanity. Somewhere along the way he came to his senses. He was repulsed by the person he was becoming. He describes it as a "rebirth" in which for the first time he saw things as they really are. Several years later, my friend came across a group that works undercover in Southeast Asia to free young girls from the sex trade. In remote rural areas, girls are kidnapped and brought to the city, where they are forced to work as prostitutes. My friend signed up and recently went undercover on a "mission," rescuing girls and helping them start a new life. I was with him when he showed a group of people a picture of him surrounded by the girls he had helped rescue. People were blown away by the picture.[15]

He's charging into hell and bringing heaven with him.

We don't respect the divine image in others just because we want to uphold their humanity. It isn't just about them.

It's about us.
It's about our humanity as well.

I just received an email asking if I would sign a petition protesting the use of torture to get information from enemy soldiers caught in battle. The email said this issue is being debated among politicians right now and that the public needs to speak up on the matter.

There's a debate about this? The issue isn't just what torture does to the person being tortured, it's what torturing does to the person doing it. We're already in trouble when people debate the use of torture as if it's only about what it does to the enemy.

Our own humanity is at stake.

The New Humanity

The first Christians had a phrase for what happens when people properly respect and acknowledge the image of God in those around them. In the letter to the Ephesians, we read about a group of people who were previously divided because of race, background, wealth, socio-economic status, worldview, and religion.[16] One group is made up of Jews, the other Greeks, and in this new church, they find themselves united because they've all become followers of the resurrected Jesus Christ. All of the old categories simply don't work anymore. This new commonality, this new bond, is simply bigger than all of the things that had previously kept them apart.

The first Christians called this the "new humanity."

In the beginning, God created us "in his image." So first, God gave us an image to bear. Then God gave us gender: male and female. Then God gave us something to do, to take care of the world and move it forward, taking part in the ongoing creation of the world.[17] Later, people began moving to different places. It takes years and years of human history to get to the place where *these* people are from *here* and *those* people are from *there.* Different locations, skin colors, languages, and cultures come much later in the human story.

What we often do is reverse the creative process that God initiated. We start with different cultural backgrounds and skin colors and nationalities, and it's only when we look past these things that we are able to get to what we have in common—that we are fellow image-bearers with the shared task of caring for God's creation. We get it all backward. We see all of the differences first, and only later, maybe, do we begin to see the similarities.

The new humanity is about seeing people as God sees them.

When They Become We

I was having lunch in September of last year with a group of people I had just met. We were discussing the kind of work we each did and places we had been, and one man started telling stories about being in the marines. He had led one of the first groups into Iraq during the Gulf War in 1991. He talked about what it was like to enter enemy territory and to be shot at—about the complexities of war—and he had us all on the edge of our seats. During one battle he and his marines won quickly, they had to arrest the soldiers who had just been shooting at them. They lined them up and were handcuffing them when one of them ran up to him waving a letter, begging to have it sent immediately. The man was frantic and starting to cause a scene. He kept repeating that this letter he was holding had to be sent immediately. He then looked the marine in the eyes and said, "Please mail this letter for me. It's to my father, and he must know that I love him."

The man telling the story paused, looked around the table at each of us, and said, "He had no idea about the troubled relationship I had with my own father. Here I am, out in the middle of nowhere in the desert of Iraq, trying to arrest a group of soldiers who moments before were trying to kill me, staring at a man who wants me to mail a letter for him, thinking, *I could be him.*"

Several years ago a woman called the church where I was a pastor because she wanted to talk. We set up a time to meet, and when she showed up, I asked her how I could help. She said that she was a prostitute and didn't want to live anymore, so she had made a plan to kill herself. She described in detail how she was going to do it, when she was going to do it, and where it was going to happen. She was very thorough. She said she was telling me all of this because she had to know whether she would go to heaven or hell when she died. Somewhere in the course of telling me her plans, she mentioned that she had a daughter because one of her clients had gotten her pregnant. She was confident that a family member would raise her daughter when she was gone.

I asked her to tell me more about her daughter. She gave a few details. Then I asked what her daughter's name was.

She replied, "My daughter's name is Faith."
Faith.

There are these moments when the enemy all of a sudden becomes just like me.

When a soldier becomes a son.
When a prostitute becomes a mother.
When they become we.

When those become us.
When he becomes me.

Moments when all of the ways that we divide ourselves and rank each other and convince ourselves of how different, better, and unalike we are disappear, and we are faced with the fact that first and foremost, we are humans. In this together. And not that much different from each other.[18]

Jew. Gentile.
Marine. Iraqi.
Orphan. Family.
Pastor. Prostitute.

We could be them.

Thirty Years Later

When I was five, my family visited my grandparents in California during Christmas vacation. They lived in an apartment building with an alley beside it—very exciting for a boy who lived on a farm in Michigan. At some point in my exploration of the alley, I decided to make a Christmas present for my dad out of the things I had found there. So on the morning of the twenty-fifth, my father had the privilege of opening a gift of a piece of black and green drainpipe glued to a flat gray rock with little white stones resting on the inside of it.

A masterpiece, to say the least.

The reason I remember this is because I visited my dad at his office a few days ago, and while I waited for him to finish his meeting, I wandered around looking at the pictures on his walls and the papers on his desk and the things on his shelves. On one of his shelves sat the drainpipe and rock sculpture, thirty years later.

He still has it.

He brought it home with him and put it in his office in 1977 and hasn't gotten rid of it.

We know why he kept it. How you treat the creation reflects how you feel about the creator.

When a human being is mistreated, objectified, or neglected, when they are treated as less than human, these actions are actions against God. Because how you treat the creation reflects how you feel about the Creator.

To be a Christian is to work for the new humanity. Jesus commands his followers to feed and clothe and visit and take care of those who need it. They're fellow image-bearers, they're just like us, and when we love them, we're loving God.

A church exists to be a display of the new humanity. A community of people who honor and respect the poor and rich and educated and uneducated and Jew and Gentile and black and white and old and young and powerful and helpless as fully human, created in the image of God.

These bonds we have with each other are why, for many, there is so much power in the Eucharist, also called Mass or the Lord's Supper or communion. We take the bread and dip it in the cup to remind ourselves of Jesus's body and blood.[19] To reflect on the truth that we're all in this together, one body, and that his body being broken and blood being spilled are for our union.

It isn't just about our relationship to God as individuals. Often communion is seen as a time to reflect on God's love for us in Jesus's dying on the cross. Which it is. But it was originally just as much about my desperate need to be reminded of your humanity and the humanity of all the people around us.

When I respect the image of God in others, I protect the image of God in me. When Jesus speaks of loving our neighbor, it isn't just for our neighbor's sake.[20] If we don't love our neighbor, something happens to us.

And in trying to protect the image of God in them, we just might be protecting the image of God in ourselves in the process. Because with every decision, conversation, gesture, comment, action, and attitude, we're inviting heaven or hell to earth.

I have a new hero. Her name is Lil, and I would guess she's in her late fifties. I met her earlier this year when she introduced me to her daughter, whom she was pushing in a wheelchair. Early in their marriage, Lil and her husband[21] decided that they would adopt two children. As they became familiar with the family services system, they learned that there were kids in the system nobody wanted. So they went to the local adoption agency and asked for the kids with the most pronounced disabilities, the most traumatic histories, and the most hopeless futures. They asked if they could have the kids nobody wanted. Over the past thirty or so years, they have raised well over twenty children, raising their biological children alongside their adopted children.

When Lil got to this point in her story, she reached down and patted her daughter and said, "This is Crystal. She's twenty-seven years old but will be about six months old developmentally for the rest of her life. She can't talk or walk or move or feed herself or do anything on her own. She will be like this, totally dependent on us, until the day she dies. And I love her so much. My family and I, we can't imagine life without her. She makes everything so much better."

What is Lil doing?
She's bringing heaven to earth.

She gives us a glimpse into another realm. Into a better way. The way of God.

She and her family have taken kids who were discarded because of their perceived lack of worth and said, "No, you are not to be rejected and turned away. We are going to love you as an equal, as a human, as one of us."

They show us how God loves us.

They reflect the image. And when you see it lived out like this, you're seeing heaven crash into earth.

Instead of seeing labels like "handicapped," "reject," or "invalid," Lil and her husband and her kids see only one label: "human."[22]

And so they have only one response: love.
And it makes all the difference in heaven and earth.

Which takes us back to something that happened during Colonel Gonin's stay at the Bergen-Belsen concentration camp:

> It was shortly after the British Red Cross arrived, though it may have no connection, that a very large quantity of lipstick arrived. This was not at all what we wanted, we were screaming for hundreds and thousands of other things and I don't know who asked for lipstick. I wish so much that I could discover who did it, it was the action of genius, sheer unadulterated brilliance. I believe nothing did more for these internees than the lipstick. Women lay in bed with no sheets and no nightie but with scarlet red lips, you saw them wandering about with nothing but a blanket over their shoulders, but with scarlet red lips. I saw a woman dead on the postmortem table and clutched in her hand was a piece of lipstick. At last someone had done something to make them individuals again, they were someone, no longer merely the number

tattooed on the arm. At last they could take an interest in their appearance. That lipstick started to give them back their humanity.

Because sometimes, the difference between heaven and hell may be a bit of lipstick.

CHAPTER TWO

SEXY ON THE INSIDE

Last year I was in Canada for a couple of days, staying in downtown Ottawa. When I got to my hotel, I noticed that there was a buzz about the lobby. Lots of people with cameras and lots of British accents.

I got my key and took the elevator to my floor, and as I walked down the hall, the door of the room next to mine opened and a woman stepped out wearing a shirt with four words on it: "Mick, Keith, Ronnie, Charlie."

Ah, yes, the Rolling Stones.

With great passion, she told me that they were staying in this very hotel and that the concert was tomorrow night, only a mile from here.

The next night, I went to the stadium and bought a single ticket from a man standing at the main gate. I found my seat and began talking with the couple next to me. At one point they asked what I do for a living. I told them that I'm a pastor.

They looked at each other, stunned. They told me that they weren't very religious or part of a church or anything like that, but on the way to the concert, they both had this unusual sense that there would be some sort of significance to whoever they ended up sitting next to that night.

We discussed politics and the environment and literature and nuclear energy and music and family—all during the opening band. At one point the woman asked why the world was so broken and why people have such difficulty getting along. The question seemed to come from years of reflection. And it wasn't just an intellectual issue; this was something that deeply troubled her soul. She pointed to the forty thousand people seated around us in the stadium and asked, "Why is it so hard for us to get along? Why do we have to fight with each other and go to war and hurt each other and sue each other and say horrible things about each other?"

As she was saying this, I realized that what she was saying was less a series of questions and more of a lament. A grieving.

We're disconnected from each other, and we know it. It's not how things are supposed to be. Even people who would say they have no faith in God or in any sort of higher being or supreme power still have a sense that there is a way things are supposed to be. And that way involves us as humans being connected with each other.

I recently talked to a woman in our church whose husband has a history of physical abuse. She told me about the group of people who have come around her to help her through her pain. They're helping her set boundaries so that she and her children are protected, offering her whatever they can in the way of resources and support.

Several weeks after talking to her, a man walked up to me with tears in his eyes and told me that he had hit his wife and he wanted to get help so he could put his life and his marriage and his family back together.

It was him.

I asked him who he had to talk to about all of this, and he said he had no one. As I stood there looking at him, I had this sense that in this one man I was seeing what is missing with so many in our world. He was made for loving, connected relationships with others, but he's cut off. Separated. Alone.

But our disconnection isn't just with each other.

The Earth and Us

My boys and I were at the beach recently searching for shells and unusual things that had floated to shore. We found a giant jellyfish (dead), hundreds of hermit crabs (alive), a baby shark (dead), and lots of starfish (which are alive but appear to be dead). We also found broken glass, pop cans, plastic bags, and candy wrappers, and at one point, when my boys ran ahead, I looked down and there at my feet was a used syringe.

We're disconnected from the earth. And we know it. Or at least we can feel it, even if we don't have words for it.

We have been given this responsibility to take care of our home, to carefully steward and order and manage it, and we're in trouble. From oil to air to pollution to wetlands, we find ourselves in our bare feet on a beach, almost stepping on a needle.

Notice the premise of many car commercials. How many of them deal in some way with getting out of the city and exploring nature? The makers of these commercials understand that we are alienated from the earth.

Many people live in air-conditioned houses and apartments.

We alter our air with electric machines.

We spend vast sums of money and energy to change our air. And we drive in air-conditioned cars—the 8 percent of us in the world who have cars—to air-conditioned schools and offices and stores with tile floors and fluorescent lights.

It's even possible to go days without spending any significant time outside.

And it's still considered living.

It's easy to go for weeks and maybe even years without ever actually plunging your hands into soil. Into earth. Into dirt.

But this car—this is the one, the one with the space for my cooler and the kayak that I don't own. This is the car that will change things.

Massive amounts of money are spent convincing us that this particular automobile will give us access to the mountains, streams, and deserts that we are unable to access at this moment. And when we make that trip, in that car, the one from the commercial, we will be connected with the earth. With our home.

We see this disconnection in the relationship between our sleep patterns and the invention of electricity.[1] Prior to the lightbulb, people generally went to bed when the sun went down and woke up when the sun came up. With the invention of electric light, sleep habits became less and less regulated by the rising and setting of the sun. As a result, people today get far fewer hours of sleep a night than people did a hundred or two hundred years ago. We even have third-shift jobs in which a person works through the night while it's dark, and then sleeps through the day while it's light. All of this affects our connection with nature. Where once the rhythm and flow of life were dictated by the rhythm and flow of the earth, we now live relatively independent of these forces.

There's no better way to understand how disconnected we are from our environment than to ask the big metaphysical question, the question that has challenged the great minds of our generation and the generations before us, the question that if we had a clear answer for it, would unlock the deepest mysteries of life on this planet:

Where *does* our trash go?

The truck comes to our place of residence, they dump into the back whatever we dumped into the approved container with the phone number and name of the company on the side, and we think no more of it.

Have you ever later in the day thought to yourself, *I hope my garbage made it there safely*?

Where is "there"? And how many "theres" are there? And what do they do with it when it gets there? Does every town have a there? Can the people who live next to there smell there? Are there laws about how many theres a town can have? Is there a point at which a there is full? How is this determined? Can the people who run the theres give us a percentage of how full their there is? Do they get together and discuss these sorts of things with other people who own theres?

No, we don't even think about it. We know that skilled, highly trained people are on the job, and so we don't spend a moment thinking about it.

Until we go camping. And the sign says to take out everything we take in. And for an hour or a day or a week, we're highly attuned to what we're doing to the environment. We pick up every wrapper, we bury everything that should be buried, we wait until every last coal is burned out. All because we don't want to pay the fine.[2]

Which of course raises the question, Is there some sort of larger fine that all of us are going to have to pay, as the human race, for our actions? And if we were aware of what that fine was going to be, would we all of a sudden care very much about "there"?

But our disconnection isn't just with each other and the earth.

Yesterday I was with a friend who recently started a new job. He had taken the job because he had a clear vision for how he could help bring significant change to the company. A few months into the job, he was exhausted. As he sat across the table from me venting about all of the ways he's frustrated and burned out and tired, something powerful began to happen. He began to remember why he took the job in the first place. He started articulating all of the ways that he had become disconnected from his original vision for the company because of the voices around him telling him how he should do his job. Right before my eyes, he rediscovered his passion for the work he was doing. He repeatedly asked me, "How did I get so off track? How did I become so disconnected from myself?"

We struggle in our connection with the earth, in our connections with each other, and with being connected with ourselves.

But it wasn't always like this.

In the Beginning

In the first chapter of Genesis, when God creates the first people, he blesses them. This is significant. God's blessing is the peace of God resting on people. The story begins with humans in right relationship—in healthy, life-giving connection—with their maker. All of their other relationships flow from the health of this one central relationship—people and God. They're connected with the earth, with each other. They're naked and feel no shame.

And then everything goes south.
They choose another way.
And they become disconnected.

God goes looking for them in the garden, asking, "Where are you?" The first humans make coverings of fig leaves, and then they're banished from the garden.[3]

Disconnected from each other.
Disconnected from the earth.

The woman is told that there is going to be conflict between her and the man. The man is told that there is going to be conflict between him and the soil.

And this is where you and I come in. We were born into a world, into a condition, of disconnection. Things were created to be a certain way, and they're not that way, and we feel it in every fiber of our being.

Is this why the first thing newborns do is cry?

We're severed and cut off and disconnected in a thousand ways, and we know it, we feel it, we're aware of it every day. It's an ache in our bones that won't go away.

And so from an early age we have this awareness of the state of disconnection we were born into, and we have a longing to reconnect.

Scholars believe that the word *sex* is related to the Latin word *secare,* which means "to sever, to amputate, or to disconnect from the whole." This is where we get words like sect, section, dissect, bisect.[4]

Our sexuality, then, has two dimensions. First, our sexuality is our awareness of how profoundly we're severed and cut off and disconnected. Second, our sexuality is all of the ways we go about trying to reconnect.

Last year I was swimming in the ocean with one of my boys on my back in the midst of a pod of dolphins. They were swimming around us and under us and making their noises, which are incredibly loud and piercing, when one of them shot up into the air above us and did a flip. Right over our heads.

When we describe moments like these, the words we use are rarely about distance. The words we use are about nearness and connection, sometimes even intimacy.

Your friends just got back from hiking, and they say, "We felt like we could just reach out and touch the mountain."

I just spent an afternoon with a doctor who donates significant amounts of time working with people who have AIDS and can't afford proper treatment. He loves it. He talked with great passion about the joy it brings him. He's a successful, educated, wealthy man who loves to spend his time with poor, uneducated people who are from a totally different world than he is. He was telling me how his work brings him a sense of connection, an awareness of the simple truth that we aren't all that different from each other.

These moments move us because they have a sexual dimension. They help us become reconnected. They go against our fallen nature, which is to be cut off.

This is why music is so powerful. Have you ever noticed that when you ask people why a particular song or concert moved them so much, they often resort to ambiguous explanations? You rarely receive a response such as, "Well, the prolific use of polyrhythms offset with the arpeggiated succession of relative minors touched my heart."

No, of course not. You get words like emotion and passion and energy and relationship and connection. Music is powerful because it is sexual. It connects us. We generally don't think of it in those terms, but it's true. The experience of a great concert—with everybody singing together, waving their hands in the air, and a feeling of oneness permeating the room—has a significant sexual dimension to it. We don't know each other, we come from vastly different backgrounds, we disagree on hundreds of issues, but for an evening, we gather around this artist and these songs and we get along. The experience moves us so deeply because it taps into how things were meant to be, and we have so few places where we can experience what God intended on such a large scale.

Whether it's a concert or a church service or a rally for a just cause, certain communal events draw us into something bigger than the event itself. We feel connected with the people we're having the experience with, and not just connected but aware of something bigger than us all that we're brushing up against in the process.

What we're experiencing in these moments of connection is what God created us to experience all of the time. It's our natural state. It's how things are supposed to be.

It's written in the letter to the Ephesians that there's "one God and Father of all, who is over all and through all and in all."[5]

And in the book of Hebrews, it's written that God is the one "for whom and through whom everything exists."[6]

Rethinking Our Definition

If we take this understanding of our natural state seriously, we have to rethink what sexuality is.[7] For many, sexuality is simply what happens between two people involving physical pleasure. But that's only a small percentage of what sexuality is. Our sexuality is all of the ways we strive to reconnect with our world, with each other, and with God.[8]

A friend of mine has given his life to standing with those who have been forgotten and oppressed the most.[9] He's in his early thirties, he's single, and he talks openly about his celibacy. What makes his life so powerful is that he's a very sexual person, but he has focused his sexuality, his "energies for connection," on a specific group of people.

Some of the most sexual people I know are celibate. They sleep alone.

They have chosen to give themselves to lots of people, to serve and give and connect their lives with beautiful worthy causes.[10] These friends help me understand why the Red Light District in Amsterdam is so sexually repressed. If you've ever walked through this part of the city, where prostitution is legal, you know that it can be a bit jarring to have the women in the windows gesturing to you, inviting you to come in and have "sex" with them.

What is so striking is how unsexual that whole section of the city is. There are lots of people "having sex" night and day, but that's all it is. There's no connection. That's, actually, the only way it works. They agree to a certain fee for certain acts performed, she performs them, he pays her, and then they part ways. The only way they would ever see each other again is on the slim probability that he would return and they would repeat this transaction. There's no connection whatsoever. If she for a moment connected with him in any other way than the strictly physical, it would put her job, and therefore her financial security, in jeopardy.

And so in the Red Light District there's lots of physical interaction and no connection. There are lots of people having lots of physical sex—for some it's their job—and yet it's not a very sexual place at all.

There's even a phrase that people use with a straight face—"casual sex." The rationale is often, "It's just sex."

Exactly. When it's just sex, then that's all it is. It leaves the person deeply unconnected.

You can be having sex with many, and yet you're alone. And the more sex you have, the more alone you are.

And it's possible to be sleeping alone, and celibate, and to be very sexual. Connected with many.

It's also possible to be married to somebody and sharing the same bed and be very disconnected. It's possible to be married to somebody and sharing the same bed and even having sex regularly and still be profoundly disconnected.

There's a saying in the recovery movement: "You are only as sick as your secrets." This is true for relationships as well. If there are secrets that haven't been shared, topics that can't be discussed, things from the past that are forbidden to be brought up, it can cripple a marriage.

And so they're sleeping together, but they're really sleeping alone.

The Communal Dimension

This has huge implications for what it means to be a part of a community. How many people do you know who aren't a part of a church, company, or community because of the way they were treated?

When we hurt each other,
when we gossip about each other,
when we fail to forgive each other,
when we don't do the work of making peace with each other,
we get severed from each other, cut off, divided.

I often meet people who aren't part of a church and don't want anything to do with God because of "all those religious hypocrites." Often they have great pain that they blame on "the church." But it's not possible for an institution, whether it's a church or a school or a business or even the government, to hurt somebody.[11]

Institutions are made up of people.
People hurt people.

Somebody in *this* group hurt somebody in *that* group. Somebody at that school or in that office wronged somebody else. And they haven't done the work to apologize and make amends and work through it. When I meet someone who has been burned by an institution, my first question is, "What was the person's name?"

We'll never heal until we can identify who did what when. Only then can we begin the process of being set free.

People who move from relationship to relationship, church to church, group of friends to group of friends, may do this because they have a hard time connecting and committing. Some people refuse to humble themselves and do the difficult work of learning how to forgive and reconcile, and so whenever a relationship hits a bump or turns sour, they leave it. They move on to the next one.

Perhaps we should call this what it is: sexual dysfunction.

A friend of mine who is celibate makes it very clear that her vow of celibacy is not to go without love, but it's a vow to what she calls "universal love." I've realized over time that she is a deeply connected person. There is a certain potency to her presence that is hard to describe. She owns no property and she lives as simply as she possibly can because she committed early in her life to give everything she had to making the world the kind of place God dreams it could be. It is a joy to be with her because everything matters in her life. Nothing is shallow or trite or superficial. She's very funny and smart and compassionate—a magnificent human. Because she's been exploring her own soul for so long, she knows herself inside and out. She's at peace, and it's contagious.

You can't be connected with God until you're at peace with who you are. If you're still upset that God gave you this body or this life or this family or these circumstances, you will never be able to connect with God in a healthy, thriving, sustainable sort of way. You'll be at odds with your maker. And if you can't come to terms with who you are and the life you've been given, you'll never be able to accept others and how they were made and the lives they've been given. And until you're at peace with God and those around you, you will continue to struggle with your role on the planet, your part to play in the ongoing creation of the universe. You will continue to struggle and resist and fail to connect.

The other day my five-year-old son asked my wife, "Mom, what does sexy mean?"

She thought about it for a second, and then replied, "Sexy is when it feels good to be in your own skin. Your own body feels right, it feels comfortable. Sexy is when you love being you."[12]

Because it all starts with being sexy on the inside.

CHAPTER THREE

ANGELS AND ANIMALS

This past year my family and I stayed at a wildlife lodge in Africa. We would wake up early each morning and climb into a Land Rover with our guide, who drove us all over the "bushveldt," as the Africans call it, looking at animals in their native habitats. Rhinos, cheetahs, giraffes, elephants, birds that had flown to Africa from Russia for the winter—we saw it all. In the afternoon of our second day, as we pulled into a large clearing, we saw two lions lying out in the open.

A male and a female.

The female would periodically get up and walk back and forth in front of the male, then she would roll on her back and side, then she would lie still for a while, then she would go through her routine all over again. Our guide explained that it was—you guessed it—mating season, and the female was going through this ritual to get the male ready for their "encounter." Our guide then launched into an extended explanation of the male-female relationship and how they attract one another and how the one relates to the other.

When you see the biological need up close, so raw and so primal, you can't help but notice how strong it is. These animals are going to mate because it's in their DNA, their blood, their environment. They aren't lying out there in that field, thinking, *I just really want to know that you love me for more than my body.* They aren't discussing how to make a difference in the world. One isn't saying to the other, "I just don't feel you're as committed to this relationship as I am."

Other than basic biological functions, there's nothing else going on.

Pure instinct.

No higher plane,
no greater cause,
no transcendent purpose.

Biology. Period.

Those lions reminded me of when I was in high school and my sister and I were visiting some relatives in Florida during our spring vacation. We decided to go check out the "scene" at Daytona Beach. I'm assuming you know the scene I'm referring to. It happens all over the place every spring. Cancun or the Caribbean or an island off the coast of Texas or whatever spot is "the spot" for that particular year is invaded by thousands and thousands of students from all over the country to drink large amounts of alcohol and have sex with lots of people.

The vibe is the same regardless of the year or the location or even the weather. This is your week to let yourself go, to lose yourself, to give in to whatever cravings or desires or urges you have. Because whatever happens in (choose a city), stays in (that city).[1]

Perhaps you've been there, you've seen the footage, or you've heard the stories. There's the pervading sense that if something feels good, it takes precedence over everything else. And so how do the stories that are brought home begin?

"I can't believe I . . ."
"We totally lost our minds . . ."
"It was so out of control . . ."
"The next morning I couldn't . . ."

These scenes aren't just about partying and having a good time and hooking up with someone, they raise questions about what it means to be fully human. The temptation is to ignore your conscience or sense of higher purpose, sacrificing what it means to be human. Which leads a person to act much like . . . an animal.

Are we just the sum of our urges?

Think about some of the phrases that get thrown around:
party animal
we attacked each other
she's a tiger
basic instinct

They're all an acknowledgment of the primal, base nature of the person's behavior. As if there are these incredibly strong forces down in there that are usually repressed but for these few days are going to be allowed to take over. And when they're given the reins, you have no idea what might happen.

Food for the Stomach

In the ancient Greek world, people used a phrase to describe this understanding of what it means to be human. They would say, "Food for the stomach and the stomach for food."[2] They understood a person to be a collection of physical needs—you're hungry and there's food to satisfy your hunger, you're tired and there's sleep. They concluded that sex is just like food, so when a man was "hungry," he would go to a prostitute, saying, "Food for the stomach . . ."

There's a passage in the book of First Corinthians where one of the writers of the Bible addresses this worldview. He confronts his audience with a challenge: Can they live for a higher purpose than just fulfilling their urges? He then claims that their bodies are "temples of the Holy Spirit, who is in you, whom you have received from God."[3]

This is provocative language. A temple was a holy place, a place where the gods lived, a place where heaven and earth met. The writer specifically uses this image to challenge them with the idea that a human isn't just a collection of urges and needs but is a being whom God resides in. He's trying to elevate their thinking, to change their perspective, to open their eyes to a higher view of what it means to be a human. He's asking them to consider that there's more to life than the next fix.

The "stomach for food" perspective continues to be a dominant worldview, even to this day. The problem with it is that it's rooted in a low view of human nature. The assumption behind it is that people are going to have sex because they can't help themselves. This perspective is presented as freedom and honesty and just being who you are and doing what comes naturally, but it's built on the belief that certain things are inevitable. What it really teaches is that people cannot transcend the physical dimensions of their existence. It views people much like animals.

And so many live with a low-grade sense of despair, thinking that they're helpless, that this is

simply
how
it
is.

Nowhere is this chronic despair more visible than in a lot of sex-education curriculums, many of which are based on the premise that "kids are going to do it." If you deconstruct that, what do you get?

A loss of hope.

Who decided that kids—or anybody else for that matter—are unable to abstain?

In a lot of settings, abstinence programs are laughed at. So are those campaigns in which students commit themselves not to have sex until they're married. Have you ever heard a news piece on the television or read a magazine article about one of them that didn't at least subtly mock the idea of "keeping yourself pure for marriage"? People who organize and promote these kinds of campaigns are often viewed as hopelessly naive messengers from a far-off land that simply doesn't exist anymore. The criticism of the "sex is for marriage" view is usually presented as the voice of realism. Are people actually capable of restraint?

But it's not realism. It's the voice of despair. It's the voice that asks, "Aren't we all really just animals?"

And Now for Angels

In the same way that we can veer toward the animal impulse, we can veer toward the angel impulse. And the one is just as destructive as the other. If the animal impulse is to give in and let our cravings rule us, the angel impulse is the opposite. It's the denial of the physical and the failure to acknowledge that our sexuality is central to what makes us human.

I recently had a conversation with a woman whose daughter has been dating a guy for several years. My friend was telling me that her daughter mentioned recently that she and her boyfriend had never kissed. Which I guess isn't *that* big of a deal. . . But then my friend went on to say that her daughter is a little disturbed because her boyfriend isn't physical with her at all. Nothing. Ever. Holding hands, you know, the basics—nada. Cold fish. And they're several years into the relationship.

My friend's daughter is starting to wonder if everything is all right with him. Which of course is leading her to a far more troubling question: Is everything all right with *her*?

Which got me thinking about a conversation I had recently with a group of friends. Somehow we got on the subject of how we were first told about sex. One friend heard about it from his dad, who used ticket stubs to show how . . . well, actually, he doesn't remember how the ticket stubs fit into his dad's explanation. He was so traumatized by the subject that he stopped listening partway through. Other than his experience, which made us laugh, and a few others, it was striking how many in the group did not hear about sex from their parents. In fact, as the conversation continued, it turned out that a good number of the group were raised in homes where sex was not talked about at all.

How can a parent ignore something this big?

A man I've known for years was recently telling me about some of his challenges running a youth camp over the past year. The biggest one involved a fifteen-year-old girl. It had recently come out that she had been having sex with a man in the area. Which, among other things, got the man in trouble with the law. But when my friend and the girl's dad got involved, it turned out that she'd been having sex with, well, lots of men in the area. My friend said that as the truth began to come out, her dad was shocked. He had no idea that she was this involved with anybody, let alone with this many men.

How can a father be that clueless?

But as many of us read that last sentence, we were thinking, *Lots of parents are that clueless.*

Parents who don't talk with their kids about sex, ever?

College students who have been dating for years who simply have no physical attraction for each other?

Think about the woman who has just gotten married and she's trying to figure out what it means to be true to her new husband and yet she doesn't want to have sex with him. She's got a million confusing messages about sexuality and obligation and love and him and her and it, and so instead of talking about it and getting it out into the open and dealing with it and learning and being open and honest she

just
stuffs
it.

And he's got images and pictures and fragments of stories floating around in his head about what a woman is supposed to be and do for him, and this woman he's just married who's supposed to do that and be that and perform a certain way simply isn't delivering. His temptation is to deal with his frustration through all sorts of other channels that will only drive the two of them farther apart.

Denying and stuffing and repressing never work because it's a failure to acknowledge what is central to being a human being.

They can pretend they're angels, but they're not. They have to talk about what they're experiencing and how they're feeling and what it's doing to them or they will begin the long slow drift apart.

Or the person who was badly burned in an unhealthy sexual relationship and became cold and withdrawn from anybody of the opposite sex. And he's been this way for years. He doesn't let himself feel. And he has essentially turned his sexuality off. You can't pretend you're an angel.

Angels and animals.

There are these two extremes, denying our sexuality or being driven by it, and then there's the vast space in between.[4]

More

In the creation poem of Genesis 1, God creates animals before humans. And something significant happens in the creation of people that doesn't happen in the creation of animals: people are created in God's image. We have a spiritual dimension to us that animals don't have. Some call this consciousness, others an awareness of "more," others call it transcendence. However it's described, the writer of Genesis wants us to see the distinction between what it means to be human and what it means to be an animal.

Have you ever seen a dog concerned that its life just isn't going anywhere?
A cat reflecting?
A horse not feeling centered?
Animals have a physical body but no spirit.[5]

In the book of Job, it's written that when God created the world, "all the angels shouted for joy."[6] And in the book of Psalms, it's written that God made humans "a little lower than the heavenly beings," which is a reference to angels.[7] The book of Hebrews says that an angel is a spirit.[8] A spirit is a being with no body, no physical essence.

Marriage and sex and procreation simply aren't parts of their existence.

An angel is a being with a spirit but without a body.

When we deny the spiritual dimension to our existence, we end up living like animals. And when we deny the physical, sexual dimension to our existence, we end up living like angels.

And both ways are destructive, because God made us human.[9]

The tension here cannot be resolved easily, if ever. In the first century in the Asia Minor city of Ephesus, there was a religious group that was aware of the powerful sexual forces that we carry within us.[10] They observed that sex can get us into lots of trouble. Which we'd probably all agree with. Their conclusion was that because sex is so dangerous, it should just be avoided altogether. But to avoid sex, you need to avoid romance and affection and all that comes with them, and of course you're going to need to eliminate marriage altogether. So this religious group forbade their followers from getting married.

They had a similar practice in regard to food. There were foods sold in the markets of the cities that had been offered to the local gods in the local temples as part of their worship rituals. The leaders of this religion decided that if something had been offered to a god they didn't believe in, they wouldn't eat it. Their response was to make lists of foods the members of their religion could and couldn't eat.

Do you see the problem with their religion? Anytime things got ethically complicated, anytime the waters got even slightly murky, anytime there was something to be held in tension, they simply avoided the issue.

Instead of dealing with the ambiguity and the lack of clarity that many things in life can bring when a person first encounters them, they would simply throw the whole thing out.

This is where the first Christians come in. One of them, a man named Paul, who wrote many letters to the early churches, addresses this issue in a letter to the Christians at Ephesus. He warns them about those who "forbid people to marry and order them to abstain from certain foods," telling them that those are things "God created to be received with thanksgiving by those who believe and who know the truth."[11]

Paul's point is brilliant. He makes a distinction between the inherent good of something and the abuse of it. People may have seriously distorted the good gift that sex is or offered food to gods that lead people into destructive ways of living, but that doesn't mean that sex or food are inherently wrong. He continues, "For everything God created is good, and nothing is to be rejected if it is received with thanksgiving, because it is consecrated by the word of God and prayer."[12]

He insists that everything God created is good, and we come to see this through what he calls "the word of God and prayer," which is the hard work of study and reflection and meditation and discussion and debate. The temptation is always to avoid things that are difficult and complex. To go around them rather than through them.

Think about the parents of a junior high girl who has just hit puberty and all of a sudden her body has changed in some significant ways, and she's being noticed in ways she wasn't before and now she's starting to notice that she's being noticed. Her parents have to talk to her about all of this. They have to wade into the complexity and confusion and mixed messages that our culture is sending their daughter. If they indulge one way, telling her to use her body to get what she needs and encouraging her to draw as much attention to her body as she can, they're encouraging her to act like an animal. But if they ignore these changes and hope the whole thing just goes away, they're sending her an equally destructive message. They're treating her like an angel. Her sexuality and her body and her beauty are good things. They were given to her by God. Her parents must embrace this and all that comes with it. And they have to teach her how to embrace it in an honorable, dignified way. They must live in the tension and then show her how to do the same.

And so Paul addresses this religious group with their narrow and restrictive lists, claiming that they are actually working against God's purposes in the world. Things that God has made, things that are good, things that God created to be enjoyed, are being ignored and avoided because these religious people refuse to live in the tension.

And now for the opposite end of the spectrum. A friend of mine recently interviewed Hugh Hefner, founder of the Playboy empire, for a book she was writing.[13] They did the interview sitting on a couch in the Playboy mansion in Los Angeles. As he answered questions about his upbringing, he said, "I was raised in a setting in which [sex] was for procreation only and the rest was sin."

What's he saying, essentially? He was raised by parents pretending to be angels.

He continued later in the interview: "Our family was Prohibitionist, Puritan in a very real sense. . . . Never hugged. Oh, no. There was absolutely no hugging or kissing in my family. There was a point in time when my mother, later in life, apologized to me for not being able to show affection. That was, of course, the way I'd been raised. I said to her, 'Mom, you couldn't have done it any better. And because of the things you weren't able to do, it set me on a course that changed my life and the world.' "

It isn't difficult to understand his reaction to an angelic upbringing. He was denied something central to what it means to be human: affection. And so the rest of his life has been a journey to the other end of the spectrum.

In reaction to denial, people often head to the other end of the spectrum, which is indulgence. The pendulum swings. But we were created to live in the tension. And when you lose the tension, you lose something central to what it means to be human.

Living like angels can be just as destructive as living like animals.

In the first-century example, the religious group understood how destructive the physical can be; in the Hugh Hefner example, Hefner saw how destructive a lack of the physical can be.

We see this back and forth in individuals, in families, in cultures, and in churches. By painting sex as this horrible thing that is unclean and of the dark side, a parent or a church or a school can make kids want to do what? Of course! Go have sex.

Getting It Out

The impulse in our world when faced with tension is to come up with the seven steps or the formula so that if you do things in the right order the tension will go away. But that doesn't always work. One of the marks of someone who has experienced significant growth in their soul is their ability to live in the midst of tension. Often people are told, "Just don't have sex and you'll be fine." Well, yes, that's true, to a certain extent. If you're talking to a room full of junior high students, they will be much better off if they learn the fine art of self-control. But it's larger than that. Because they are still full of raging hormones. Much like the rest of humanity. To simply tell them to ignore the animal and be the angel puts them in the awkward place of trying to ignore something that is very real and very new, something central to who they are.

We have to talk about everything we're experiencing. Repressing and stuffing and refusing to acknowledge never works. Whether it's a friend or a group of peers or a priest or a pastor or a counselor, we have to get it out.[14] Some friends of mine started a website where people could talk about their struggles with their sexuality, and right away it received several hundred thousand visitors.[15]

Several hundred thousand.

You are not alone. Whatever you struggle with, whatever you have questions about, you are not alone. It doesn't matter how dark it is or how much shame or weakness or regret it involves, you are not alone.

Some say the struggle is about *eros,* which is where we get the word erotic. Others call it testosterone and blame it on hormones. The Greeks called it the madness of the gods. The truth is, we're crammed full of sexual energy. It's how we're made. We have cravings and desires and urges and temptations that can easily consume us and make us feel helpless in their presence. We have to talk about what we do with the forces that rage within us. We have to get it out or we will begin to die on the inside.[16]

Some of the most comforting words in the universe are "me too." That moment when you find out that your struggle is also someone else's struggle, that you're not alone, and that others have been down the same road.

Tohu Va Vohu

Which takes us back to the beginning, to Genesis and the angels and the animals, which were both created before humans. We're told in the first chapter of the Bible that God created all of this out of chaos. The earth was formless and void, and God brought order out of it. The Hebrew phrase for this formless and void state is *tohu va vohu.* Some translate the phrase "wild and waste." Each thing God creates and sets in motion is a step, a progression away from the chaos and disorder toward order and harmony. The first things God commands these people to do, then, involve the continuation of this ordering and caring for and the ongoing progression away from chaos.

The universe isn't finished.

God's intent in creating these people was for them to continue the work of creating the world, moving it away from chaos and wild and waste and formlessness toward order and harmony and good.[17] As human beings, we take part through our actions in the ongoing creation of the world. The question is, What kind of world are we going to make? What kind of world will our energies create? We will take it somewhere. The question is, Where?

Either we're acting in ways that move the world away from the *tohu va vohu* or we're contributing to the chaos and lack of order.

In the creation poem that begins the Bible, people are created *after* animals. And from the rest of scripture, we learn that people were also created after angels. The order here is significant. The movement in creation is away from *tohu va vohu* toward greater and greater harmony and order and beauty.

Angels were here before us.
Animals were here before us.

When we act like angels or animals, we're acting like beings who were created *before* us. We're going backward in creation. We're going the wrong way. We're headed back toward the chaos and disorder, not away from it.

Our actions, then, aren't isolated. Nothing involving sex exists independent of and disconnected from everything around it. How we act determines the kind of world we're creating.

I remember a story in the news about a group of college athletes who hired two dancers to perform at a party they had. The party ended with allegations of rape, and from there the story became about race and power and money and economics and status and all sorts of other things. It was a big mess. But what kept coming up was that these particular athletes had a well-established reputation for being out of control. Their parties were legendary. So their defense, even if it was solid and true, had this cloud over it because of how they were known to behave. And the administration of their school was in the awkward position of wanting to deal with this nightmare but really just wanting the whole thing to go away. But instead they had to keep explaining why they hadn't done anything in the past to deal with the—let's call it what it is—animal behavior of their athletes.

And as a result this university was in chaos.

Because God has left the world unfinished. And with every action, we're continuing the ongoing creation of the world. The question is, What kind of world are we creating?

How we live matters because God made us human.
Which means we aren't angels.
And we aren't animals.

CHAPTER FOUR

LEATHER, WHIPS, AND FRUIT

If the Bible were made into a movie, there are lots of parts I wouldn't watch.

Too graphic, too much detail, excessive violence. You'd think God would have gone for a more family-friendly rating, something Christians could recommend that their friends go see, but instead we have a book crammed full of shocking stories about people doing unbelievably destructive things.

Genocide, polygamy, incest, cutting people up into pieces and mailing the chunks to different parts of the country—and that's just the first few books. I find one scene in particular almost unreadable. It's in Second Samuel, a history book that records the reign of King David. One of David's sons, Amnon, falls in love with his sister Tamar.

And that's just the first verse of the chapter.

The text says that Amnon became "so obsessed with his sister Tamar that he made himself ill."[1] Amnon's advisor notices his steadily declining mood, and after hearing of his frustration, the advisor proposes a plan. The plan involves Amnon telling his father, David, that he's sick and wants Tamar to bring him food.

When Tamar comes in, Amnon orders his servants out of the room and tells Tamar to come to bed with him. She resists, begging him not to harm her. The text reads, "But he refused to listen to her, and since he was stronger than she, he raped her."

Now we could spend hours discussing the evils of what happens when a man uses his strength to harm, threaten, or coerce a woman. We could reflect on the horrors of abuse and incest, the tragedy that family members are able to inflict on each other.[2] The silence of King David. The list goes on.

But notice the next verse: "Then Amnon hated her with intense hatred. In fact, he hated her more than he had loved her."

What an odd thing for the writer to tell us. The last thing you would expect to hear is how Amnon is feeling, let alone that he feels hatred. We understand her repulsion, but his?

What is it about rape that provokes such disgust in him?

"He hated her more than he had loved her."

What is it that makes Amnon go from one extreme to the other?

He gets what he wants and it makes him . . . angry? What is it that turns him so fast?

What is it about that line "more than he had loved her" that doesn't ring true?

It's lust.

Lust can drive us to do frightening things. It can own us, it can take up massive amounts of head space, and it can make us miserable.

And once in a while, lust may even have something to do with sex.

A Tree with a Long Name

In the beginning, in the opening pages of the Bible, we find God creating all sorts of trees.[3] They're good for food and pleasing to the eye, and God wants them to be enjoyed. God creates this garden and places people in the middle of it because God wants these people to enjoy it. The word God uses for this is "good." It's all good from God's perspective.

But for it truly to be good, it can't be forced upon these first people. That wouldn't be good. It has to be their choice. And so there's a tree in the middle of the garden called the tree of the knowledge of good and evil.

A bit long for the name of a tree, but the idea is that there is another way for these people to live, outside of how God designed things. And if they eat the fruit of this particular tree, they'll see what that other way is like, a way separated from the life of God.

And so we have a man and a woman in a garden, eating a piece of fruit. The text puts it like this: "When the woman saw that the fruit of the tree was good for food and pleasing to the eye . . . she took some and ate it."[4]

We're told that the fruit engages her senses:

she sees
she notices
she appreciates
she takes
she eats

Her sight, her touch, her senses of smell and taste are all involved.

Our senses are incredibly strong.

Maybe it's her perfume
or the feel of that fabric
or how these have a particular shape and form
or what it feels like to open a package of those.

Smoking isn't just about nicotine, is it? It's about opening a new pack, the feel of the paper, the smell of the cigarette. Fishing isn't just about fish. It's about the rocking of the boat and the morning air and what's in the cooler. Shopping isn't just about new clothes. It's about the tags and the fabrics and the sound of the hangers sliding on the rack.

We are sensory creatures.

My brother just got a new Apple computer. Several of us were there when he opened it, and we were so into it that we were actually handing the various parts around the room. If you have taken part in this particular ritual, then you know that Apple ships everything in white and silver bags and liners that would make dirt look attractive. We were even passing the power cord around the room, admiring its design.

Were we losing our minds? The power cord?

The designers at Apple understand something significant about what it means to be human: we are hardwired to appreciate sensory experience.[5]

Texture, shape, color, feel, aroma.

The things God creates in Genesis are "pleasing to the eye." We have an ingrained sense of appreciation for how things look and feel and smell because God has an appreciation for how things look and feel and smell. We bear the image of our maker.

The problem for Adam and Eve isn't the food. There's nothing inherently wrong with the food. The food is good. This is what Eve notices about it, that it's "good for food." It's created by God for the enjoyment of people. The same goes for most of the things and people we lust for. In most cases, there's nothing wrong with them inherently—

her body,
that product,
this food.

The problem for Adam and Eve is what the fruit has come to represent. Rebellion against God. Rejection of the good, the true, and the beautiful. Another way.

This is really about that.

If I Just Had . . .

The appeal to Eve's senses comes with a promise that the fruit will deliver something it can't—specifically, a better reality than the one God has made. The problem isn't the fruit. It's what is promised through the fruit—that she won't die if she eats it. The problem is that she's told, "When you eat of it . . ." and then she's told things that aren't true. Promises are made to her that the temptation can't come through on. It's a lie.

Lust promises what it can't deliver.

By giving in to the temptation, Adam and Eve are essentially claiming that God isn't good. They're giving in to the deception that good is possible apart from God, the source of all good. The scriptures call this being separated from "the life of God."[6] When these first people eat the fruit, it isn't about the fruit, it's about their dissatisfaction with the world God has placed them in.

Creation isn't good enough for them.

From their perspective, their place in the midst of it isn't good enough. And so they eat the fruit and everything falls apart. They're tempted with something that promises what it can't deliver, and they live with the consequences.

Lust comes from a deep lack of satisfaction with life. This is why we have to slow down and reflect on our lives before we'll ever begin to sort out the significance of this. Lust often starts with a thought somewhere in our head or heart: "If I had that/him/her/it, then I'd be . . ."

When we're not at peace, when we aren't content, when we aren't in a good place, our radar gets turned on. We're looking. Searching. And we're sensory creatures, so it won't be long before something, or somebody, catches our attention.

And it always revolves around the "if," doesn't it?

If I just . . .

The idea creeps into our head and heart that we are lacking, that we are incomplete, that this craving in front of us is the answer.

The "if" means we have become attached to the idea that we are missing something and that we can be satisfied by whatever it is we have in our sights.[7] There's a hole, a space, a gap, and we're on the search. And we may not even realize it. When we are in the right place, the right space—content and at peace—we aren't on the search, and our radar gets turned off.

Adam and Eve fixate on this one piece of fruit from this one tree when God has given them endless trees with infinite varieties of fruit to enjoy. Which is often our problem. There's so much to enjoy, and yet we fixate on something we don't have.

This is why gratitude is so central to the life God made us for. Until we can center ourselves on what we do have, on what God has given us, on the life we do get to live, we'll constantly be looking for another life. That is why the word *remember* occurs again and again in the Bible.[8] God commands his people to remember who they are, where they've been, what they've seen, what's been done for them. If we stop remembering, we may forget. And that's when the trouble comes.

Head Space

Lust is always built on a lie. And so for you and me to be free from lust, we have to begin by understanding the lie and where it comes from and why it can be so alluring.

The word *lust* in the Greek language is the word *epithumia.* It's actually two words in Greek: the word *epi,* which means "in," and the word *thumos,* which refers to "the mind."

In the mind.

Think about the head space we give to things and people we want. It's easy for our thoughts to be dominated by a craving. We're in a meeting, we're taking a walk, we're studying, we're doing jobs around the house, and the whole time our brain is miles away, trying to figure out how to get it.

It takes ahold of us.
We are not free.
Lust is slavery.

If I want something to the point that I can't conceive of being content without it, then it owns me.

One writer in the scriptures puts it like this: " 'I have the right to do anything'—but I will not be mastered by anything."[9]

That last part is great, isn't it? "I will not be mastered by anything."

We are free to do anything we want. But because I can doesn't mean I should. There is a massive distance between "can" and "best."

We're addictive creatures. We try things, we experiment, we explore, and certain things hook us. They get their tentacles in us, and we can't get away from them. What started out as freedom can quickly become slavery. Often freedom is seen as the ability to do whatever you want. But freedom isn't being able to have whatever we crave. Freedom is going without whatever we crave and being fine with it.

Where It Leads

In the book of Ephesians, the writer claims that we get enslaved to lust because we become "darkened" in our understanding. The passage explains that we're separated from the life of God because of ignorance due to the hardening of our hearts.[10]

It isn't just what lust does, it's where lust leads. God made us to appreciate aesthetics: taste, smell, touch, hearing, sight. Shape, texture, consistency, color. It all flows from the endless creativity at the center of the universe, and we were created to enjoy it. But when lust has us in its grip, one of the first things to suffer is our appreciation for whatever it is we're fixated on.

The scriptures call this "having lost all sensitivity."[11]

The word *insensitivity* is the Greek word *apalgeo.* It comes from the root word *algeo,* which means "to feel pain," and *apo,* which means "lacking or going without." It's the condition of being void of or past feeling. We could translate the phrase in Ephesians as "having lost the ability to feel things like they used to."

Addictions often rob people of their appreciation of things.

An alcoholic may have once enjoyed the taste, but now he is using drinking to numb and escape and avoid, and the last thing he's reflecting on is the quality of the brew or the vintage of the grapes.

And she used to appreciate food—the spices and the aromas and the art of cooking—but now her taste buds have dulled. She no longer savors every bite. She has lost her enjoyment of food as a gift from God that comes from the earth for our pleasure and sustenance. Her addiction, her turning to food for what it can't deliver, has caused her to have contempt for food, and so she's losing sensitivity.

There's a progression here. The loss of sensitivity and enjoyment often leads to what the scriptures call being given over to sensuality.[12] The Greek word for *sensuality* is *aselgeia.* It's the absence of restraint, an insatiable desire for pleasure. When our lusts get the best of us, they trap us. Whether it's food, sex, shopping, whatever, what was supposed to fill the hole within us didn't. It betrayed us. It owns us. And it always leaves us wanting more.

And so we're
emptier
lonelier
hungrier
more depressed.

"He hated her more than he had loved her."

And so we go to the refrigerator and eat the whole box.
We go to the website and watch every clip.
We buy one in every color.
We take another.

And then we're right back where we started. We're momentarily satisfied, and then we experience letdown because it didn't deliver what it promised.

Which of course leaves us wanting more. The passage in Ephesians calls it "greed"—the word *pleion* in Greek, which means "more," combined with the word *echo,* which means "to have."

We have to have more.
But when we get more, it leads to . . . more.

Lust does not operate on a flat line, as if we can give in and stay at the same level of consumption indefinitely. People who are not aware of what they're dealing with will keep insisting that they're fine and that they can stop at any time. But they're "darkened in their understanding." They're operating under the assumption that lust can plateau at a certain level and simply stay there. But lust always wants more.

Which is why lust, over time, will always lead to despair. Which will always lead to anger.

Lust always leads to anger.

Sometimes it isn't expressed on the outside because it turns inward. That's depression. When it goes outward, it will often affect what a person indulges in—darker and darker expressions of unfulfilled desire mixed with contempt. Is that how someone ends up at leather and whips?[13]

Food or clothes or position or approval or power or sex—it grabbed us and said, "You are missing out until you have me." And it was a lie. It promised us something. It claimed to be the answer.

But it wasn't.

Lust says to us, "If you just had this, everything would be fine."

But it's not true. We wouldn't be okay, and we have closets full of clothes to prove this. We thought that shirt and those pants would change the way we feel about our bodies, about how others perceive us, about how comfortable we are in our own skin. And then we got them and nothing changed, except the size of our bills.

Lust promises what it can't deliver.[14]

Dark to Light

To be free from lust, we have to move from being darkened in our understanding to being enlightened in our understanding. And to be enlightened, we have to ask lots of questions about the things we crave:

What is this craving promising?
Can it deliver?
Is this lust about something else?
What is the lie here?
Where is the good in this person or thing?
Where is the good that has been distorted?
What good thing has God made here that has been hijacked?
Have I been tempted like this before?
Have I given in before?
What was it like?
Did it work?
Was I more satisfied or more empty?
What will the moment, the morning, or the week after be like?

Is there a pattern here?

Maybe the most powerful thing we can do is simply to pray, "God, give me eyes to see the lie here."

Perhaps you can relate to this progression and the lie and the ways we get hooked. Maybe you know exactly what I'm talking about because you're in the middle of it right now. Something has got its tentacles wrapped around you, and you are having an impossible time getting free.

Happens all the time.

And so it feels like it's you versus the craving. You against the addiction. Your brain and heart against your flesh.

I often meet people who say, "My battle against . . ." and then they name something that has them in its grip.

To be honest, if it's us against the craving, we will often lose. It's too hard. And what happens most of the time is we see ourselves fighting all alone against some temptation that is so strong it wins. Maybe we will win here or there, but those become the exceptions. And when we give in, it can start to feel pointless. Why resist today if tomorrow we won't be able to?

There's Something Else Going on Here

There's a passage in the book of Ephesians where it's written, "Those who have been stealing must steal no longer."[15]

Which is quite straightforward—don't steal. But the passage doesn't end there. It continues: "but must work, doing something useful with their own hands."

But it doesn't there. It ends with: "that they may have something to share with those in need."

On first read, the instructions seem as basic as it gets. But there is much going on here just below the surface.

First, the command doesn't stop with the "don't" part. The writer understands that that kind of instruction rarely helps. When we're told not to do something, how often are we truly compelled not to do it, especially if we enjoy it? If it's just me against the lust, the odds are already against me.

But there's something else going on here.

Stealing involves large amounts of adrenaline. The rush of planning, pulling it off, not getting caught, getting something for nothing. And then there's the expectation of next time. If we got something this significant for free, could we steal something even more valuable? What if we raised the stakes, hit a store with a better security system, tested ourselves? Stealing involves the senses, the intellect, a person's fear threshold. It even has a powerful social dynamic. Stealing with someone creates powerful bonds between people. When our adrenaline is pumping, that's a physiological phenomenon. It feels good because things are happening with the chemicals in our bodies, with our nerves and brain and bloodstream. If we do that enough, our bodies get used to it.

We could use the word addicted. A person gets addicted to it.

If you tell the person who's stealing not to, and you leave it at that, you've taken something away, but you haven't replaced it with anything. That's why the instructions in Ephesians are so brilliant. The urging to stop stealing is followed by the command to have the person do "something useful with their own hands." The word *useful* is the Greek word *agathos,* which is also translated "good" and "benevolent."

Why does the writer mention the hands?

Because you steal with your hands. Stealing is a sensory experience, an adrenaline rush involving the hands. The command is to replace one adrenaline rush with another, a better one, one that's good. But it doesn't stop there. The command ends with the person who was stealing learning to do something good with their hands so that they can take care of the needs of someone else. Stealing is about taking from someone. This passage is about giving to someone who has less because you have more.

Stealing is the ultimate in being selfish.

Making something and giving it away is the ultimate in being generous.

This passage is about something central to what it means to be human: it's about desire. It's about the thief finding something they'll desire more than stealing.

"You thought taking things for free was a rush? Try giving free food to someone who's starving."

The writer of Ephesians understands that to tell the thief not to steal and leave it at that doesn't have a very high chance of being helpful. The thief will be left with a battle on their hands that will pit them against their craving.

Whatever it is that has its hooks in you, you will never be free from it until you find something you want more. It's not about getting rid of desire. It's about giving ourselves to bigger and better and more powerful desires.

What are you channeling your energies into?[16]
Because they will go somewhere.

If they don't go into a few, select, disciplined pursuits that you are passionate about and are willing to give your life to, then they'll dissipate into all sorts of urges and cravings that won't even begin to bring the joy that the "one thing" could.

You are crammed full of the "madness of the gods." And you will end up giving the force of your being to something.

Maybe it's as simple as asking God to show it to you, to give it to you, to make you aware of it.

There was a story all over the news about a television star whose boyfriend videotaped the two of them having sex and then put it on the internet. Apparently lots of people were watching it, and she was crushed. Which is sad. But what's tragic is that she was known for having sex and shopping. It kind of became her schtick—she was making a career out of being shallow. Now, of course, she was all over the media, and she was making lots of money, so she was clearly much smarter than she let on, but she was made for so much more than this.

Her life force was tremendous. But the problem was she hadn't channeled it into something, or a few things, that were good and true and beautiful. She hadn't focused all of that God-given sexual energy into the ongoing creation of a better and better world. And so she fell for all of these temptations that robbed her of the joy she was made for.

The last thing she needed to do is tone down those energies.
She simply needed to redirect them.

What is it you've given your life to?

Life is not about toning down and repressing your God-given life force. It's about channeling it and focusing it and turning it loose on something beautiful, something

pure and true and good, something that connects you
with God, with others, with the world.

What do you want more?

How can you make your life about *that* so that you won't
be tempted to give in to *this*?

CHAPTER FIVE

SHE RAN INTO THE GIRLS' BATHROOM

When I was twelve, I went to a dance at my school. It was held in the cafeteria, where they folded up the lunch tables and brought in a DJ. The girls stood on one side of the room, the boys stood on the other. Every once in a while, somebody would bravely venture across this massive chasm to ask someone to dance, and then everybody would watch them. Perhaps you endured this particular form of torture at some point in your adolescence.

It is not pretty.

I remember walking up to a girl, whose name I can recall with clarity twenty-four years later, and asking her if she would like to dance with me. Those of you who have walked this road know the determination and fortitude it takes to leave the boys' side, walk across the lunchroom-turned-dance-floor to the girls' side, and make your request. It takes all that a young man has in him not to buckle under the enormity of the pressure. But I did it. I made it to the other side and asked her if she would like to dance with me.

Her response?

She burst into tears and ran into the girls' bathroom, where she spent the rest of the evening.

Strange the things we remember, isn't it?

But perhaps there's a reason certain stories stay with us years later. It's not just that they're true in that they actually happened, but they're true in the sense that they point to something else, to larger truths about how life is.

When I asked this girl to dance, I gave her the choice of saying yes or no. I gave her options. If she had said yes, all sorts of new possibilities would have opened up, namely my getting to dance with her. And then maybe another dance. And then maybe a phone call the next week. Perhaps passing some notes in class. Whatever it is that twelve-year-olds do in a "relationship."

But if she said no, then things weren't going to progress at all. And this was her decision, not mine. By extending myself to her in the invitation to dance, I took a great risk. I risked that she would say no and I would be left standing there on the girls' side of the cafeteria humiliated.

Which is what happened.

I had to live with her decision.
I was at the mercy of her choice.
I had given her the power in the relationship, at least what there was of a relationship.

When you make a move toward a person, when you extend yourself to them,
when you invite them to do something,
when you initiate conversation,
you give them power.

Power to say yes or no.
Power to decide.

This is true from junior high dances to marriage proposals to inviting someone for coffee.

Everyone who has ever received a no knows exactly what I'm talking about.

The Invitation to Risk

Anytime we move toward another in any way, we are taking a risk. A risk that she may say no. Our gesture may not get returned. Our invitation may be rejected. Our love may not be reciprocated.

A few years ago I was on a trip with a friend, and we had just gotten on the plane and sat down and fastened our seatbelts, and the flight attendant was just about to tell us how to . . . fasten our seatbelts, when my friend leaned over to me and asked, "Remember that business trip I took to the East Coast a few weeks ago? Well, it wasn't for business. I went to be with this woman I've been emailing."

But he wasn't done.

"And remember when my wife went out of town last weekend? I wasn't alone in my house. The woman I've been emailing came and spent the weekend with me."

Where do you go from there, when a friend drops a bomb like that? Needless to say, the trip had a dark cloud over it. I begged him on the return flight to leave the airport and go straight home and be honest with his wife. I promised to help find a counselor to guide them through this mess. But as I was saying goodbye to him, I realized I had a question that was more important than anything we had talked about. I asked him if he wanted to be married to his wife.

He said no.

As he said no, I had flashbacks of their wedding ceremony, the vows, the "till death do us part" section, all the friends and family who had been there. The dresses, the flowers, the toasts. The kiss.

So he went to his home, I went to mine. I had been back probably fifteen minutes when there was a knock at the door. I opened it, and there stood his wife, sobbing. She was trying to talk, but not much was coming out. She came in and sat on the couch between my wife and me, and we put our arms around her and she cried and she cried and she cried.

There are a lot of different ways to cry. There's the "somebody close to you is dying" cry, the "confessing dark secrets" cry, the "I'm angry and want to kill or at least significantly maim someone" cry, the groom's "my bride is coming down the aisle" cry, the "kid whose feelings have been hurt" cry. There's the "car accident I could have died in but didn't" cry. There's even the "I just hit my thumb with the hammer and it hurts so much but I'm not going to cry, so little tears are forming in the corners of my eyes" cry. But her cry on that day was a kind of crying I have seen many times. It's the cry of someone who has had their heart broken by a lover.

It comes from someplace else.

Someplace far inside a person, deep in the soul. It's a cry with a certain ache. It's the ache of a broken heart.

Behind the Wall

For thousands of years, the poets have known that love is risky. There's a scene in the Song of Songs, a collection of poems in the Bible, where the woman sees her lover, whom she calls her "beloved," and he's coming toward her. She says, "Look! Here he comes, leaping across the mountains, bounding over the hills."[1]

But when he makes it to her house, he can't get in.

She says, "There he stands behind our wall, gazing through the windows, peering through the lattice."

In the days these lines were written, people were often married as teenagers, so this courtship we're reading of is probably between high school students. Kids.

Which explains the "our wall" part. She's still living at home. She's under her parents' roof. She's living with her brothers and sisters and probably her extended family—aunts and uncles and cousins and grandparents.

Her life is safe. Predictable. Her family provides for her. Her father and her brothers protect her.

And what is this chap saying to her? He says, "Arise, my darling, my beautiful one, come with me."

He's inviting her to a new life. A life with him.

He continues,

"See! The winter is past;
the rains are over and gone.
Flowers appear on the earth;
the season of singing has come,
the cooing of doves is heard in our land.

The fig tree forms its early fruit;
the blossoming vines spread their fragrance."

And then he repeats, "Arise, come, my darling; my
beautiful one, come with me."

He reminds her that it's that time of the year. The time of
new life, new growth, sprouting, budding, blooming. It's
as if he points to the explosion of spring going on all
around them in nature and says to her, "This could be us!"

So much potential, adventure, possibility. This could be
us! Come with me!

This guy doesn't give up, does he? You at least want to
give him points for trying. Especially the part about the
doves. Gentlemen, try saying "cooing" with a straight
face. You gotta hand it to the fella.

But enough about his invitation. Do you see the terrifying
spot this puts her in?

Does she leave? Does she go to the door in the wall and
walk through it to the other side?

Because it isn't just a wall, it's a way of life. If she says yes
to his offer, she's trading what she knows for the
unknown.

What if it doesn't work out?
What if he isn't who he appears to be?
What if he's making this pitch to girls all over town?

What if he hits her?
What if he goes to war next year and doesn't return, ever?

This could all blow up in her face.

What if her family doesn't think he's right for her, and she goes anyway and it doesn't work out? How agonizing would it be for her to hear from her relatives for the rest of her life, "I told you so"?

Love is risky.

If she decides to love him, she runs the huge risk that she might have her heart broken.

And this risk does not end with marriage, with going through the wall and leaving home.

Later in the Song of Songs, it appears that this couple is married. He comes to her at night. "Open to me . . . my darling . . . my head is drenched with dew, my hair with the dampness of the night . . ."[2]

Now there is all sorts of commentary by scholars on what is going on here, but the general belief is that he's been gone—farming, fighting, traveling—doing something that has brought him back in the middle of the night. Normally he would stay somewhere else rather than wake her up. But he returns to their bedroom and knocks.

She responds, "I have taken off my robe—must I put it on again? I have washed my feet—must I soil them again?"

What's interesting about her words is that they translate from the Hebrew language, "I have a headache."[3]

This is the awkward, real-life stuff that happens every day in relationships. She's tired, and getting out of bed right now seems like such a hassle. It's been a long day, she's exhausted. Her reaction is, "Anytime but now."

But then she catches herself. Like we all do. Do you ever have those moments when you hear yourself talking, almost from outside of your body, and the second you finish, you're already starting the next sentence, which is, "I'm sorry, I didn't mean that. Please forget I said that. What I meant was . . ."?

She says, "My heart began to pound for him. I arose to open for my beloved . . . but my beloved had left; he was gone."

And then she adds, "My heart sank at his departure."

She's too slow, and he's gone. He extended himself, he risked, he called to her from the other side of the door, and he got a no.

Who doesn't know this feeling?

She discovers that he's split, and she says, "I looked for him but did not find him."

Now she's the one risking, searching, trying to find him. And coming up empty.

The heart has tremendous capacity to love, and to ache. And this ache is universal.

Universal Sisterhood

You can put women from all over the world with nothing in common in a room together and they may not have a thing to talk about until one of them says, "And then he cheated on me," and instantly you have universal sisterhood.

Think of the poems, songs, plays, movies, novels across the ages that have dealt with this pain. Everybody understands it.

Think about some of the great country songs, the classics. There's "She Ripped My Heart Out and Stomped That Sucker Flat," and there's "I Sure Do Miss Him, but My Aim Is Improving," and then there's my personal favorite, "Here's a Quarter, Call Someone Who Cares."

What do they have in common?
Heartbreak.

Someone got their heart broken by someone else. And now they are singing about it. And we can all relate. Even if the music gives us a rash.[4]

Why is this? And why is it that it's not just about lovers, it's about parents and their children, friends who have been hurt by friends, business partners who part ways. Why is heartbreak so universal?

It's universal because we're feeling something as old as the world. Something God feels.

The Bible begins with God making people who have freedom. Freedom to love God or not to love God. And these people consistently choose not to love God. It's written in Genesis 6:6 that God "regretted that he had made human beings on the earth, and his heart was deeply troubled."

Another translation reads, "Then YHWH [God] was sorry that he had made humankind on earth, and it pained his heart."

These ancient writers saw God as having a heart.[5]

That feels.
That responds.
That hurts.
That fills with pain.

God . . . grieving.
And what is the source of this grieving?
People.

People God had made who have freedom. Freedom to love anybody they want. And freedom not to love anybody they want. God takes this giant risk in creating and loving people, and in the process God's heart is broken.

Again and again and again.
Divine heartbreak.

For some, this is an entirely new perspective on God. Many of the popular images of God are of a warrior, a creator, a judge, a system of theology, a set of absolute truths, a father, the writer of an owner's manual.

But a *lover*?

A lover whose heart has been crushed, and expresses it in . . . poetry?[6]

This raises questions about what is at the base of the universe. What, or maybe we should say who, is behind it all?

A list of rules?

A set of beliefs, which you either believe or you don't, and if you do, you're in, if you don't, you're out?

A harsh judge and critic, who's making a list and checking it all the time?

An impersonal energy such as fate, destiny, luck, chance, or the force that you can tap into if you know the code or the technique or the philosophy?[7]

The story the Bible tells is of a living being who loves and who continues to love even when that love is not returned. A God who refuses to override our freedom, who respects our power to decide whether to reciprocate, a God who lets us make the next move.

Love Is . . .

Love is handing your heart to someone and taking the risk that they will hand it back because they don't want it. That's why it's such a crushing ache on the inside. We gave away a part of ourselves and it wasn't wanted.

Love is a giving away of power. When we love, we give the other person the power in the relationship. They can do what they choose. They can do what they like with our love. They can reject it, they can accept it, they can step toward us in gratitude and appreciation.

Love is a giving away. When we love, we put ourselves out there, we expose ourselves, we allow ourselves to be vulnerable.

Love is giving up control. It's surrendering the desire to control the other person. The two—love and controlling power over the other person—are mutually exclusive. If we are serious about loving someone, we have to surrender all of the desires within us to manipulate the relationship.

So if you were God—which I realize is an odd way to begin a sentence—but if you were God, the all-powerful creator of the universe, and you wanted to move toward people, you wanted to express your love for the world in a new way, how would you do it?

If you showed up in your power and control and might, you would scare people off. This is what happens at the giving of the Ten Commandments.[8] The first two commandments are in the first person: "You shall have no other gods before *me*. You shall not make for yourself an image . . . for *I*, the Lord . . ." But starting with the third commandment, someone else is talking: "You shall not misuse the name of the Lord *your* God, for the Lord . . ." The rabbis believed that this is because God was speaking directly to the people in the first two commands, but they couldn't handle it. As it says in the text, "They trembled with fear. They stayed at a distance and said to Moses, 'Speak to us yourself and we will listen. But do not have God speak to us or we will die.'"[9] So, the rabbis reasoned, the switch in person is because Moses gave them the remaining eight commandments.

Just God speaking is too much to bear.

If you're God and you want to express ultimate love to your creation, if you want to move toward them in a definitive way, you have a problem, because just showing up overwhelms people.

You wouldn't come as you are.
You wouldn't come in strength.

You wouldn't come in your pure, raw essence. You'd scare everybody away.
The last thing people would perceive is love.

So how would you express your love in an ultimate way? How do you connect with people in a manner that wouldn't scare them off but would compel them to want to come closer, to draw nearer?

You would need to strip yourself of all of the trappings that come with ultimate power and authority. That's how love works. It doesn't matter if a man has a million dollars and wants to woo a woman, if she loves him for his money, it isn't really love.

If you were an almighty being who made the universe and everything in it, you would need to meet people on their level, in their world, on their soil . . . like them.

This is the story of the Bible. This is the story of Jesus.

The Upside-Down Empire

Consider the story just for the sheer poetry of it.
Jesus is born to teenage peasants under questionable circumstances. His mother gets pregnant before marriage.[10] He's born amid the dung and straw of a stable. He's placed in a feeding trough.[11] His brothers and sisters think he's out of his mind,[12] and after his first sermon in his hometown, the people he grew up with form a mob and try to kill him.[13]

And who does Jesus identify with? The outcasts, the people of the land who aren't good enough, clean enough, wealthy enough, and pure enough to be a part of the establishment. He's invited to dine with the elite and the rich, which he does numerous times, but he also eats with the lowest of the low—and he enjoys it. He enjoys *them.*

He touches people with infectious skin diseases,[14] he lets questionable women touch him,[15] he lays his hands on dead bodies,[16] and he engages in conversation with promiscuous women alone in the middle of the day.[17]

His entire life is about the stripping away of power and control. Jesus always chooses the path of love, not power.

Inclusion, not exclusion.
Connection and solidarity rather than rank and hierarchy.
Touch rather than distance.
Compassion rather than control.
He comes on a donkey, not a horse.[18]
Weeping and broken, not proud and triumphant.[19]

This path Jesus has chosen, which he continues to choose day after day, takes on some ominous undertones. He finds himself at odds with those in power. Partway through the Gospels—the accounts of his life—he starts dropping hints that this path he's on is going somewhere. Somewhere that involves suffering and even death. His hints, which start turning into predictions, are about a conflict that he sees as inevitable.[20] A conflict between love and controlling power.

As we read the Gospels, we find Jesus's message putting him more and more in conflict with the religious and political leaders of his day. He's threatening their power. This is what love does, it threatens the empires of power and control and wealth and manipulation.

He's eventually arrested and put on a sort of trial, at which he's asked to perform miracles. He refuses, knowing that a display of his miraculous abilities would not be true to the path he's on.[21] He's eventually beaten and flogged. When he doesn't fight back, he's mocked, and he doesn't say anything in return. He's hung on a cross and says, "I am thirsty."[22]

Naked.
Bleeding.
Vulnerable.
Thirsty.

He even quotes a well-known prayer of the day, which includes the haunting line, "My God, my God, why have you forsaken me?"[23]

It was explained this way in a popular first-century hymn, recorded in the book of Philippians: "[Jesus] who, being in very nature God, did not consider equality with God something to be used to his own advantage; rather, he made himself nothing."[24]

Strength and Weakness

This is not weakness as we think of weakness. Jesus knows exactly what he's doing. There is a weakness that is truly weakness, that has nothing else to it—no depth, no intention, no greater purpose. But Jesus is intentional in what he's doing. His vulnerability is for a purpose.

There is a weakness that is actually strength.
And there is a strength that is actually weakness.

Take, for example, a parent who yells at their children and holds them accountable for all sorts of random tasks they were supposed to have known to do and who allows their mood to dictate the mood of the whole house. This kind of parent dominates their family with manipulative behavior and petty punishments that create chaos and insecurity for those around them. This kind of parent is using their strength, but they are actually weak. They do this because in truth, they're broken, confused, and insecure. They have no idea what they're doing, as a parent or as a person.

The same is true for managers and bosses and teachers and anyone who uses their position of authority to coerce or manipulate or bully others. They can get people to do what they want, but it's only because of the position they hold. Their authority is rooted in nothing larger or stronger or higher than their rank. And that can be taken away tomorrow. They may appear strong, but they are actually weak.

Contrast this with people who appear weak but are actually quite strong. It's when someone says something mean or cutting about us and everything within us wants to one-up them with an even nastier comment in return, thus winning the exchange, but we hold our tongue. We "lose" the round, but what we did took tremendous strength. And it would take even more strength to forgive them and then maybe even love them. It would all appear quite weak to the observer, unless they understood that what they were witnessing was actually strength in action.

It takes quite a spine to turn the other cheek.
It takes phenomenal fortitude to love your enemy.
It takes firm resolve to pray for those who persecute you.[25]

This isn't true just on an individual, relational level. It's true for families and people groups and even nations. Consider Ghandi, who is famous for his commitment to nonviolence. Think about what he accomplished. A short, bald man from India wearing a white robe and spectacles stood up to the British Empire.[26]

And won.
Without a gun.

This appeared at the time to be incredibly weak, but history teaches us, in this and many other cases, that there is a better way.

It's a way that may appear weak, but it is actually strong.

Take, for example, the Roman soldiers who flogged, mocked, beat, and then nailed Jesus to the execution stake. Soldiers in the army, earning a decent wage, spending another day at work in the far reaches of the empire, taking care of another Jew who has caused some sort of ruckus about rules and rituals and religion that makes very little sense to a sophisticated Roman. These soldiers exercise power over Jesus in killing him, but it's hollow and ungrounded strength. They are serving no greater cause than their masters' conquering more lands and building larger armies and gaining more power and wealth. The whips and hammers and nails and stakes are in the service of no greater ideal than simple human greed. It is, in the end, pointless.

Jesus is calling all of this into question. He sees it for the lie that it is and is willing to go the whole way to resist it. Including his own death. He is confronting an entire system of rank and exclusion and hierarchy that says some people are better than others and some people are worth more than others, and some are good enough for God and some aren't, and some should triumph while others suffer at their expense.

In Jesus's public exposure, he exposes the lie of the empire.

In Jesus's vulnerability, he shows how vulnerable the "strength" of power and corruption really are.

In Jesus's thirst, he shows us how greed will always leave us thirsting for more.

In Jesus's emptiness, he shows us how empty the way of the world really is.

It's all upside down: an obscure Jewish rabbi challenging a world-dominating regime, and yet several days later, rumors spread that's he's risen from the dead.

Perhaps this is why one of the soldiers at his execution starts to believe. He sees the two paths laid out before him. And in the midst of the blood and tears and suffering, he gets a glimpse of a better way.[27]

If there is a God who loves us and has acted in history to express that love, what would it look like?

This is what I mean by the sheer poetry of the Jesus story. Jesus is God coming to us in love. Sheer unadulterated, unfiltered love. Stripped of everything that could get in the way. Naked and vulnerable, hanging on a cross, asking the question, "What will you do with me?"

Me Too

This is why for thousands of years Christians have found the cross to be so central to life. It speaks to us of God's suffering, God's pain, God's broken heart. It's God making the first move and then waiting for our response.

If you have ever given yourself to someone and had your heart broken, you know how God feels.

If you have ever given yourself to someone and found yourself waiting for their response, exposed and vulnerable, left hanging in the balance, you know how God feels.

If you have ever given yourself to someone and they responded, they reciprocated with love of their own, you know how God feels.

The cross is God's way of saying, "I know what it's like."

The execution stake is the creator of the universe saying, "I know how you feel."

Our tendency in the midst of suffering is to turn on God. To get angry and bitter and shake our fist at the sky and say, "God, you don't know what it's like! You don't understand! You have no idea what I'm going through. You don't have a clue how much this hurts."

The cross is God's way of taking away all of our accusations, excuses, and arguments.

The cross is God taking on flesh and blood and saying, "Me too."

This can transform our experience of heartbreak. Instead of being something that distances us from God, causing us to question, "Where are you?," we can see that every poem by a lover spurned, every song sung with an ache, every movie with a gut-wrenching scene, every late-night conversation and empty box of Kleenex are glimpses into the life of God.

Our first need is not for people to fix our problems. People who charge in and have all the answers and try to make things right without first joining us in our pain generally annoy us, or worse yet, they push us away. They have nothing to give us. The God that Jesus points us to is not a god who stands at a distance, wringing his hands and saying, "If only you'd listened to me."

This is the God who holds out his hands and asks, "Would you like to see the holes where the nails went? Would that help?"

It's the place we find out we're not alone, where we find strength to go on. Not a strength that comes from within ourselves but a strength that comes from God. The God who keeps going. Who keeps offering. Who keeps loving. Who keeps risking.

A God who knows what it's like.

The cross is where we present our wounds to God and say, "Here, you take them."

Our healing begins when we participate in the suffering of God. When we don't avoid it but enter into it, and in the process enter into the life of God. When we see our pain not as separating us from but connecting us to our maker.

And in this connection, there's always the chance we'll find a reason to risk again.

If God can continue to risk, then maybe we can too.

Perhaps you have had your heart broken by somebody. You risked and extended and offered yourself, and they rejected and turned away and didn't return your love.

There is something divine in your suffering.
Somebody divine in your pain.
You know how God feels.
Really good, loving people get hurt. It's how things are.

Maybe you're living in the wake of a relationship that fell apart. You have to dig those moments up. The parts that hurt and the awkward conversations and the anger and the failure and the misunderstanding and the betrayal. You have to dig them up and acknowledge them before you are ever going to heal.

The danger is that you will decide it isn't worth it. Why risk if it's going to hurt like this? The tragedy would be for you to shut down, to allow a wall to be built around your heart, and for something within you to die.

A decision not to risk again is a decision not to love again. They go together.

Why is it those we love the most are the ones capable of hurting us the most? Our greatest wounds rarely come from strangers. They probably come from an ex-fiancé, a former friend, a roommate, a sister, a business partner.

Even in healthy relationships, an offhanded comment or a rolling of the eyes can cripple us for days or years or even a lifetime. This is because the more we open ourselves up, the more vulnerable we are. The more exposed we are, the more it hurts. The more we let someone in, the greater the risk. Surprise, anger, shock, betrayal, helplessness—it all gets mixed in together.

There's a phrase that I have heard used to explain how God loves everybody equally. People say that "the ground at the foot of the cross is level." The idea is that God has no favorites, that no matter where you're coming from and what you've done and who you've been with and how badly you've screwed it up, the cross is the place where God looks past it all and forgives and accepts and wipes the slate clean.

It's a beautiful idea, really.

So the statement works as a truth about God's power. God's power to liberate and cleanse and forgive and grant new life, new hope, new mercy. God's power to take something that appears hopeless and redeem it. But the statement could also be seen in a totally different light.

The ground at the foot of the cross is level for God too.

In matters of love, it's as if God has agreed to play by the same rules we do. God can do anything—that's what makes God, God. But God can't do everything. God can't make us love him—that's our choice.

Love is risky for God too.
Which is a bit like a boy asking a girl to dance.[28]

CHAPTER SIX

WORTH DYING FOR

Do I have to go on?

Several years ago I was talking with the man who was repairing my car, and he mentioned that he had a girlfriend. I asked him how they met and how long they'd been together. He said that she lived in another state and they had just met in an internet chat room. I was thinking, *Oh please, like there is any chance of this ever going anywhere.*

Today, eight years later, they are happily married with two kids.

But back to the start of my story. They began "dating," and then she packed up and moved to our city to be near him. They decided to get married, I agreed to do the ceremony, and we all agreed that my wife and I would do the premarital counseling.

In one of the sessions, we were talking about serving our spouses and taking care of their needs and putting them first, and he said, "I just don't know if I can do this." We began to probe as to why the discussion, which seemed so clear, was so hard for him. After some discussion and questions and probing, he finally said that he knew what the problem was.

"I just love mountain biking."
Which wasn't exactly what we were expecting him to say.

As we began to sort it out, he said that he was terrified that if he got married, his wife might not let him buy new mountain-bike gear and ride the trails near where they were going to live.

As always, this is really about that.

The word that came to my mind at that moment was the word *submit*.

Not her submitting to him.
Him submitting to her.
He didn't know if he could submit. Because submitting is serious. Submitting is difficult.
And it's the only hope a marriage has.

I'm aware that I am using a volatile word here, one that's been used to cause great harm to women and consequently marriages and even men. The danger is that in reaction to the abuses and distortions of an idea, we'll reject it completely. And in the process miss out on the good of it, the worth of it, the truth of it.

The word *submit* occurs only a couple of times in the Bible, most notably in the letter to the Ephesians, chapter 5. The section begins in verse 21 with the command, "Submit to one another out of reverence for Christ."[1]

The word *submit* is the Greek word *hupotasso,* and it's actually two words stuck together: the word *upo,* which means "under," and the word *tasso,* which is translated "to place in order." To submit means "to place yourself under, to give allegiance to, to tend to the needs of, to be responsive to." Some scholars believe it originated as a military term, in the sense that when soldiers submit, they place themselves under their commanding officer. The passage says we are to place ourselves under one another out of reverence, or respect, for Christ. This reference to Jesus calls us to follow his example, his sacrifice, his giving his life for ours. As it's written in the book of John, "For God so loved the world that he gave his one and only son."[2] At the heart of the worldview of a Christian is the simple truth that people are worth dying for.

I was in New York City last week and took some friends to see Ground Zero. It's hard to explain what it's like to be there. A haunting sadness seems to linger in the air. But the actual site where the towers collapsed is not the most powerful thing for me about visiting the site. What moves me is to walk several blocks in any direction and pass the firehouses, where there are memorials to the firefighters from those neighborhood stations who lost their lives climbing up the towers to save people. Why do the flowers and plaques and mementos out on the sidewalk stir us like they do? Why do we hear stories of people risking their lives to save others and we often tear up, even if we don't know any of the people involved?

Because people are worth dying for. We know it to be true deep in our bones. And when we see someone actually do it, it's overwhelming.

Jesus said in one of his teachings that there's no greater love a person can have than to lay down their life for another.[3]

We know this to be true.
People are worth dying for.

The You's Are Plural

So the teaching of the passage in Ephesians is to love and serve the people around you, placing their needs ahead of your own, out of respect and reverence for Jesus, who gave his life for us, the ultimate act of love and sacrifice. Die to yourselves, so that others can live. Like Jesus.

This passage is being written to a church, to a group of people. The "you" here is plural, meaning many people are being addressed with these words. This church is being taught how to live together in such a way that when people observe their lives together, they will see what Jesus is like.

In Greek, the passage continues with verse 22: "Wives, to your husbands as to the Lord."

Did you notice that a word is missing?

We're missing a verb. The word submit is not in the verse. You have to go looking for the verb, which is in the verse before it.

The wife isn't commanded to do anything different from what everybody is commanded to do in the previous verse, namely submitting. Placing the needs of others ahead of her own, especially in her most significant relationship—the one with her husband.

Verse 23 is next: "For the husband is the head of the wife as Christ is the head of the church, his body, of which he is the Savior."

The word *head* is the word *kephale* in the Greek language. We could spend hours analyzing exactly what it means, but the larger point is that the husband is supposed to be like Christ. And what does that look like?

Notice how the text continues. Verse 24 repeats the submit command, and then verse 25 reads, "Husbands, love your wives, just as Christ loved the church and gave himself up for her."

Christ's "headship" comes from his giving himself up for the church.

His sacrifice.
His surrender.
His willingness to give himself away for her.
His death.

Whatever authority the word *head* carries with it is rooted in the sacrifice of Christ, and therefore the sacrifice of the husband.

So the husband is commanded to lay down his life for his wife, and the wife is commanded to submit to her husband, but they're both commanded to submit to each other because everyone is commanded to submit to everyone else, and all of this is out of "reverence for Christ."

Will You?

Head spinning yet?
There's a lot here, and it centers around a paradox.

Several years ago, I met with a couple who had been married a short time and needed some spiritual direction. Their marriage was falling apart, and the week before, in the midst of a heated argument, he had hit her. As you can imagine, the meeting was tense from the start. It soon degenerated into an argument between them, with their voices getting louder and louder and their words getting more and more hurtful. At one point the husband got so angry that he looked at me and said, "Do you see what I mean? She won't submit!"

To which I replied, "Will you?"
Which didn't exactly calm him down.

He wanted her to submit, whatever that means, without his having to die. He was essentially waiting for her to obey him, as a dog would, and then his will would be accomplished. I have seen this countless times in marriages. The husband has some warped idea that he is supposed to be the leader, which means she's supposed to do what he says. And then he gets frustrated when things don't go his way. And in some cases, he actually uses verses such as these in Ephesians as his reason why things aren't working.

But none of that is what this text is all about. The husband's waiting for the wife to submit is actually a failure to lead. He thinks he's the strong leader, but he's actually weak and misguided. If he really thinks he's the head, then he would surrender his desires and wants and plans. He would die to his need to be in control and do whatever it takes to serve her, to make sure she has everything she needs. He would die to himself so that she could live.

He would lay down his life for her, like Jesus laid down his life for the church.

This is submitting to one another out of reverence for Christ.

How would she respond if it were crystal clear to her that her husband was placing her needs ahead of his own?

What if he had a habit of this?

What if she knew without a shadow of a doubt that his love for her was so great that he would give his life for her in the blink of an eye?

There are those who say, "Well, yes, that's nice now and then, but what about the tough decisions? What happens when push comes to shove and somebody has to call the shots and make the tough decisions? What then?" I've actually had this encounter several times with men after I've taught on the man dying for the woman. It's interesting how emotional men get when this verse is talked about. And "push comes to shove" is probably not the best way to frame the question . . .

Think about your friendships, the closest ones, the ones that have gone the distance. How often do you ask who is in charge? Do you ever find yourself questioning, "Where does the buck stop?"

No, it's not even on the radar. Over time you've built up reserves of trust and love, and power and control become irrelevant. The healthier and more whole a marriage relationship is, the less you ask these kinds of questions.

When people are truly living in what's called "mutual submission," you lose track of who's in charge.

In a marriage, you're talking about power and control only when something central to the whole relationship has fallen apart.

And once again, poetry comes to our rescue.

The woman says in Song of Songs, "I am my beloved's and my beloved is mine."[4]

Which Is It?

She speaks a paradox. Two things are going on here. She's giving. Giving herself away. Letting go. Losing herself in her lover. And yet she's also getting something in return: the other person. Her lover, at the same time, has let go and fallen into her. There is something about losing yourself to another and their losing themselves in you at the same time that defies our ability to categorize. Healthy marriages all have this sense of mutual abandon to each other. They've both jumped, in essence, into the arms of the other. There is a sense of mutual abandon between them. If one holds back, if one refrains, it doesn't work.

We see this again in First Corinthians, where it's written, "The husband should fulfill his marital duty to his wife, and likewise the wife to her husband. The wife does not have authority over her own body but yields it to her husband. In the same way, the husband does not have authority over his own body but yields it to his wife."[5]

So which is it?
Is his body hers, or her body his?
Who has the authority in this passage?
The only proper answer is yes.
Which is it? Yes.

"I am my beloved's and my beloved is mine."

But this paradox of mutual submission is only one of the profound things going on in this passage. The command to the husband is to love your wife "just as Christ loved the church." On the first pass, it seems quite straightforward. But as we've seen before, words in the Bible are often loaded. In this case, the word *love* in the Greek language is a specific kind of love.

The word for *love* here is the word *agape* (ah-GAH-pay).[6] We find the word all over the New Testament, and it's generally used in the context of God's love for people, as in John 3:16: "For God so loved the world."

So the man is to love the woman, to "agape" her, like God "agapes" the world.

Agape is a particular kind of love. Love is often seen as a need, something we get from others. Agape is the opposite. Agape gives.

I was talking last week with a couple whom I've known for about four years. The wife has cancer. It came on strong, she received treatment, it came back, she received more treatment. If you have been down the cancer road yourself or with someone you're close to, you know what I'm talking about. A roller coaster. Often when I run into this couple, they give me an update on how she's doing, how their last visit to the doctor went, what the latest test scores were. She's amazing—the strength of her spirit, her faith—but I'm always struck as well by his attitude toward her. His body language, the way he looks at her, his involvement with the doctors and the tests and the procedures—you can't be around the two of them for very long before you become convinced he'd take the cancer for her if he could.

Agape.

Imagine a wife whose husband isn't the man she wishes he was. He lets her down, again and again and again. She begins to withdraw, to retreat, and to hold his failures against him. If they are even capable of discussing the problems between them, often she will have a list of things she wishes he did. And so this puts him in an awkward position. If he does the things on the list, she won't know why he's doing them. Because it just comes naturally? Or because he's trying to score points with her? From her perspective, his motives are unclear. And so she develops a scorecard, usually subconsciously.

If he's good, she comes near, but if he fails, she stays at a distance. Her affection, her actions, and ultimately her love become conditional. Not agape.

Agape doesn't love somebody because they're worthy. Agape makes them worthy by the strength and power of its love.
Agape doesn't love somebody because they're beautiful. Agape loves in such a way that it makes them beautiful.

There is a love *because,* love *in order to,* love *for the purpose of,* and then there is love, period.[7] Agape doesn't need a reason.

Pulled into the Future

It's written in the book of Romans that Christ died "while we were still sinners."[8] And in the letter to the Corinthians, it's written, "Think of what you were when you were called."[9] And the prophet Jeremiah is told that God knew him and set him apart before he was born.[10]

Jesus reminds his disciples, "You did not choose me, but I chose you."[11]

People in the scriptures essentially are loved into their futures.[12] Think of how many of us had encouraging or affirming or inspiring words spoken to us years ago about our worth, our value, our future, and how those words shaped us. We often carry those words of agape around with us our whole lives.

What if that woman, the one with the husband who constantly disappoints her, what if she treated him as if he already were the man she wishes he was? What if she agapes him exactly as he is, today, with all of his flaws? If you are him, which is more motivating: being reminded of all of your failures and shortcomings, or being loved as if you're a great man?

This idea that we can be pulled into our futures appears throughout the Bible. Often the writer Paul starts with the underlying theology and foundation and then works his way to the practical examples of how to actually live these beliefs out every day. The book of Ephesians follows this pattern, with a compelling twist. The first three chapters are full of statements about who these Christians are, what their true identity is as followers of Jesus. Paul tells them they're blessed, chosen, predestined, given, redeemed, forgiven, included, marked, been made alive, saved, raised up, seated with, created, brought near; they are fellow citizens, they are members, they are being built together.

It's verse after verse of description of who they are in God's eyes. For three chapters, Paul goes on about who they already are, what's already been done for them, what's already true. He doesn't give his readers one command for the first half of the letter. He doesn't tell them to do anything. He tells them who they are and speaks to them of their identity in Christ.

It isn't until chapter four that anybody is told to do anything. Paul lays it out in this order because our understanding of how God sees us will shape everything about how we live. What we do comes out of who we believe we are.[13]

Agape shakes us. It's too good to be true.
Or maybe you could say it's good enough to actually be true.
It affects how we live, how we act, how we think about ourselves.
For God so agaped the world . . .

And so the man is commanded to agape the woman with the same kind of love that God has for all people everywhere.

It's a big task the man is given, and it's reflected in the number of words in the passage. In the Greek, the command for the woman is 47 words long, while the commands for the man are 143 words long. The onus here is on the man to love with the kind of love that will go all the way to death if it has to.

What if she were loved like this?
Do you realize that you are worth dying for?

You don't need to give yourself away to someone who won't give himself to you. You don't need to use your body to get what you need. It's a cop-out for not being a certain kind of woman—a woman of dignity and honor.[14]

Some women only know how to relate to men by making a series of transactions. They want to be wanted, and the man wants, well, the man wants what lots of men want. So they trade. Essentially they strike a deal with men, time and time again.

I have what you want, and you have what I want, so let's make a deal. I need this, you need that.

Some women learn at an early age how to negotiate. They need to be loved, to be validated, to be worth something, and they discover that by giving a little of themselves to a boy, they get what they need in return. It's a cycle, a pattern that can stay with them their entire lives.

Sex becomes a search. A search for something they're missing. A quest for the unconditional embrace. And so they go from relationship to relationship, looking for what they already have.

This search is about that need.

But sex is not the search for something that's missing. It's the expression of something that's been found. It's designed to be the overflow, the culmination of something that a man and a woman have found in each other. It's a celebration of this living, breathing thing that's happening between the two of them.

Do You Realize?

You don't need a man by your side to validate you as a woman. You already are loved and valued. You're good enough exactly as you are. Do you believe this? Because it's true. You have limitless worth and value. If you embrace this truth, it will affect every area of life, especially your relationship with men.

You are worth dying for.

Your worth does not come from your body, your mind, your work, what you produce, what you put out, how much money you make. Your worth does not come from whether or not you have a man. Your worth does not come from whether or not men notice you. You have inestimable worth that comes from your creator.

You will continue to be tempted in a thousand different ways not to believe this. The temptation will be to go searching for your worth and validity from places other than your creator.

Especially from men.

But you don't have to give yourself away to earn a man's love. You're better than that. You're already loved.

When you give too much of yourself away too quickly, when you show too much skin, you're not being true to yourself.[15] When you dress to show us everything, then in some sense we have all shared in it, or at least been exposed to it. There is a mystery to you, infinite depth and endless complexity.

As the woman says in Song of Songs, "My own vineyard is mine to give."[16] In the ancient Near East, a "vineyard" was a euphemism for sexuality. She is saying that she doesn't give herself to just anyone. She is fully in control of herself, and she is not cheap and she is not easy.

Your strength is a beautiful thing. And when you live in it, when you carry yourself with the honor and dignity that are yours, it forces the men around you to relate to you on more than just a flesh level.

You are worth dying for.[17]

If you're dating someone, what kind of man is he? Does he demonstrate that he's the kind of man who would die for you? What is his posture toward the world? Does he serve, or is he waiting to be served? Does he believe that he's owed something, that he's been shortchanged, that he's gotten the short end of the stick, that life owes him something? Or is he out to see what he can give? Does he see himself as being here to make the world a better place?[18]

These are the big questions that you need to ask yourself.

Take him to a family reunion. Do some sort of service project with him. See how he interacts with people he doesn't like.

Does he have liquid agape running through his veins?

A friend of mine was engaged to a man, and some of her friends were not excited about them getting married. As the wedding day approached, one of her friends decided to say something to her. He said, "When a woman is loved well, she opens up like a flower."

She broke off the engagement soon afterward. In one brilliant sentence, her friend taught her what agape is and what it isn't.

What does he expect of you? Does he expect you to sleep with him when he hasn't committed to you forever? Does he want all of you without his having to give all of him?

Can you tell him anything? Is he safe? Can he be trusted?

Can you open up to him, allowing yourself to be vulnerable, knowing that he will protect, not exploit, that vulnerability?

Are you opening like a flower?

When you live in your true identity, when you find your worth and value in your creator, when you live "in Christ," in who you really are, you force him to rethink what it means to be a man.

Perhaps this is why the text talks about the man dying for the woman. This can be terrifying for a man. Committing to a woman for life is going to demand courage, fidelity, and strength he may not know he has. This is why some men take such pride in their sexual conquests. They're desperately running from their fear that they don't have what it takes to lay down their lives for a woman. Sleeping with lots of women gives them the feeling of being a man without actually having to be one.

Underground Girl

I was in London last year, riding the subway, and it was crammed with people. There was a group of kids, probably fifteen or sixteen years old, standing in the middle of the train. They were paired off—I think there were three couples. Or perhaps they were starting a local chapter of the happy hands club. They were all over each other. The couples, that is.

One of the girls in particular was fascinating to watch. It was clear that she loved being loved. Or whatever you would call teenage obsession. Her boyfriend was full-on groping her in the middle of a Tuesday afternoon in public, and it was clear to the rest of us on the subway that she was thoroughly enjoying it.

What was intriguing was the look on her face. She was so happy. And the happiness was obviously directly tied to her boyfriend.

What drives a girl to give herself to a boy at such a young age? What does she believe about herself? About him? About sex? About her worth?

What if she said to her boyfriend, "I'm interested in your character, your integrity, your honor—I want to find out what you're made of. Are you brave? Are you courageous? Would you fight for me?"

What if she said, "I'm not going to sleep with you anymore because I want to know what, exactly, our relationship is based on"?

What if subway girl demanded that before she gave herself to subway boy, he had to prove that he was the kind of man who would lay down his life for her?

Would subway boy still want to be with subway girl? Because she's worth dying for.

Which takes me back to mountain-bike man sitting in my living room. He got it. It clicked. He came to this realization that if he was going to marry this woman, he had to take a leap. He had to jump. He had to trust that this mysterious paradox called mutual submission really is a beautiful thing to behold. He had to have faith that if he gave himself to this woman, all of himself, it would be worth it.

She would be worth it.
Because she's worth dying for.

And as far as I know, he still rides his mountain bike.

CHAPTER SEVEN

UNDER THE CHUPPAH

It is such a letdown to rise from the dead and have your friends not recognize you.

Several years ago a kind-of-famous female singer married a kind-of-famous man-in-a-boy-band singer. This would not have been significant news except for the fact that the manager of the kind-of-famous female singer, who happens to be her father, had an idea. What if cameras recorded the first year of their marriage, and then the footage was edited into half-hour television episodes? How close could the cameras, and therefore the rest of us, get to their marriage?

The show was a huge hit, making this kind-of-famous-as-individuals couple incredibly famous—for being married.

I watched an episode and was riveted. It was kind of like that feeling you get when you pass a bad car accident and you look at the wreckage, only it lasted a half hour. And if you watched it, you were riveted too. Even if you deny it.

The two of them discussing sandwich meat.
The two of them arranging the clothes in their closets.
The two of them riding in a car together, looking out the window.

Enthralling television.
Two people famous for being married.

And then I was in the airport several weeks ago, and as I walked by a newsstand, who's on the cover of half the magazines on the rack? The two of them, with the title above their picture: "Split."

I stood there looking at those magazine covers, sadly thinking, *Too many people under the chuppah.*

Chuppah?

The first time I saw a *chuppah* (HOO-pah), I was in Israel, sitting on the balcony outside my hotel room, when I saw that a wedding ceremony was going on right below me. I noticed that the bride and groom were standing under some sort of canopy or sheet, and that it covered only them. It looked like someone had attached a beach towel to four sticks.

Standing under the chuppah is an ancient marriage tradition with roots in the book of Exodus, when the Hebrew people were in slavery in Egypt. God says, "I have heard the cry of my people."[1] These words are central to understanding the God of the Bible. God is the God of the oppressed, the poor, and the enslaved. There are over 2,100 verses in the Bible dealing with the poor and the oppressed. God is on their side. Always. God hears their cry. Some call this God's preferential option for the poor.[2]

Exodus begins with the God of compassion, the God of justice, hearing the cry of slaves in Egypt and setting out to do something about it. God sends a man named Moses to rescue them, and it's through Moses that God makes four promises to these slaves.[3]

"I will take you out."
"I will rescue you."
"I will redeem you."
"I will take you to me."

There's a reason why these four promises are so significant—they're the promises a Jewish groom makes to a Jewish bride. This is wedding language. Somebody hearing this story in its original context would realize that some sort of marriage is going to take place.

The next fourteen chapters anticipate the coming marriage between these newly liberated Hebrews and this God of the oppressed.

The marriage of God and people.
The union of the divine and the human.

What they learn is that the desert is a very, very hard place to live.

It's hard to find food
and hard to find water
and hard to defend against enemies
and hard not to grumble that maybe they were better off
in their old life.

The writer wants us to see that God is with these people.
In their grumbling and complaining and ingratitude, God
is with them. The text says that a "cloud by day and a fire
by night were with them all the time."[4] The Hebrew word
here for the presence of God is *Shekinah.* The Shekinah of
God, hovering over his people in a cloud and in fire.

God tells them, "Now if you obey me fully and keep my
covenant, then out of all nations you will be my treasured
possession."[5] "Treasured possession" is the phrase a
groom would call his bride. More wedding language.

The response of the Hebrews is, "We will do everything
the Lord has said."[6]

The people essentially say, "We do."

Then God says to Moses, "Go to the people and
consecrate them today and tomorrow. Have them wash
their clothes and be ready by the third day, because on
that day the Lord will come down on Mount Sinai in the
sight of all the people."[7]

So Moses does this. The text then adds this detail: "After
Moses had gone down the mountain to the people, he
consecrated them, and they washed their clothes. Then

he said to the people, 'Prepare yourselves for the third day.'"[8]

Ketubah

The key word here is *consecrate.* In Hebrew it's the word *qadhash,* which means "to set apart, to separate for something sacred." The third day comes, there's thunder and lightning and a thick cloud covers the mountain, and Moses leads the people out to meet with God. God then speaks the words of the Ten Commandments.

Now, often the Ten Commandments are seen as the harsh rules of a God who is looking for ways to judge and control people. Just follow the rules and no one will get hurt. As if the best that God can come up with is a list of things people shouldn't do. Often religion with this understanding of God has very little to say to people beyond "don't do this and don't do that."

But the Ten Commandments are about something else. In a Jewish wedding ceremony, a legal document called the *ketubah* must be agreed upon and signed by both parties. Essentially it's a list of what they are entering into. Both the bride and groom must be clear with each other on what they are committing to, what they both affirm it will take for this relationship to work.

The Ten Commandments are the *ketubah*. They're the agreement between the people and God about how they're going to live together, which is why the first one deals with having other gods. It's essentially an agreement that this relationship won't work if they have other lovers.

And for the rest of the Hebrew scriptures, we find God referring back to these original vows. In the book of Hosea, God says to his people, "You cheated on me!"[9] The whole book is a picture of how God's people have been unfaithful to him. In one text God laments, "You were the bride of my youth."[10]

This was supposed to be a beautiful thing, but the people haven't been faithful. They've broken God's heart.

From the perspective of the scriptures, then, a man and a woman coming together is a picture of God and his people coming together—the God of Exodus, the God who travels with his people in a cloud of smoke and fire. The God who is with his people. The God of the Shekinah.

To symbolically represent this coming together, for thousands of years Jews have taken a prayer shawl, which in the book of Numbers God commanded the people to wear, and fastened the four corners to four poles, and then the wedding attendants hold the four poles so that the couple can exchange their vows under the canopy, the chuppah.[11] A marriage takes place under the chuppah just like Israel exchanged vows with God under the Shekinah. This same God, the one who hovers over his people, hovers over a married couple, protecting them and journeying with them and blessing their union.

A marriage is a sacred, holy thing. And the Shekinah glory of God rests upon it.

In the ancient world, after the *ketubah* had been signed and the vows had been exchanged, the couple still wasn't officially married. There was one important act that made them married.

Their physical union.

So the wedding party would lead them to their bridal chamber, attach the chuppah above their bed, leave them, and the couple would consummate their relationship.

With all of the guests waiting outside.

When the woman says in the Song of Songs, "Let the king bring me into his chambers," this is wedding language. There's a celebration about to start.[12]

Then the couple would come out, and the celebration would begin. Now that they've had sex, they're married. And the celebration would be massive, often lasting for days. Lots of wine. Lots of dancing. Lots of singing and stories and laughing. Jesus attended a wedding where the host ran out of wine. The party had already been going on for a while, and yet it wasn't over. Jesus wants it to continue, so he turns some water into more wine. We're told that he does it with "six stone water jars, each holding from twenty to thirty gallons." If you do the math, that's somewhere between 120 and 180 gallons of wine.

A bit more than cake and a punch bowl on a Saturday afternoon.

Sex Is Marriage?

Let's go back for a minute to the "now that they've had sex, they're actually married" part. Because central to the celebration of their marriage is the celebration that they are sexual beings. And central to their union is their sexual relationship. Everybody at the celebration knows that they've had sex because they sat outside and waited.

Their understanding is that sex is not an optional thing for a marriage, something couples can take or leave. The sexual bond is central to what it means to be married.

No consummation, no marriage.

This understanding of sex as marriage is found throughout the Bible because it was thought of this way throughout the ancient world.

In Exodus 22 the command reads, "If a man seduces a virgin who is not pledged to be married and sleeps with her, he must pay the bride-price, and she shall be his wife."[13] If this seems barbaric, it gets even more extreme in Deuteronomy 22: "If a man happens to meet a virgin who is not pledged to be married and rapes her and they are discovered, he shall pay her father fifty shekels of silver. He must marry the young woman, for he has violated her. He can never divorce her as long as he lives."[14]

Obviously we're repulsed by the inhumane treatment of women in these passages, and at first glance it seems there's nothing remotely redeeming about these laws. But the Bible was always ahead of its time. Women basically had no rights in the ancient Near East. A man could do anything he wanted to her. He could rape her and then be on his way. He was free from the consequences of his actions. And a woman who had been raped was considered violated and unclean and would often be considered unworthy to be anyone's wife. But this passage essentially says to the man, "You want to have sex with her? Then you must take her as your wife, take care of her, provide for her needs, fulfill your duties as a husband to her. She is your equal, and you will treat her as such."

This passage is a giant leap forward. Not the final leap, obviously, and we still have a long way to go, but in that day, at that time, it was much-needed progress. The Bible doesn't stop here. By the New Testament, things have progressed so far that men are being commanded to lay down their lives for women.

God meets people where they are and invites them to the next stage of enlightenment. And then, when they've reached that stage, God invites them to the next stage after that.[15]

The point of the Deuteronomy and Exodus passages? Sex, in the ancient world, was marriage. If you had sex, you were married. All that needed to be worked out was the legal and financial consequences of what this man and this woman had just done. The physical union was what, in the eyes of society, made them man and wife. At the wedding, then, the party didn't start until they had sex.

Which is a bit different than in our culture. Sometimes when a couple is living together, one of their friends tells them they should make things right in God's eyes by making their relationship a legal marriage. But maybe it's already a marriage in God's eyes, and maybe their having sex has already joined them as man and wife from God's perspective.

This isn't a low view of sex, it's a higher view of sex. It's a higher view of marriage. It's people living in the reality of the decisions they've already made.

Back to the wedding. What exactly is it that goes on under the chuppah?

Whatever it is, it's a powerful, sacred, holy thing. It has to be respected at all costs. Often people are unaware of just how serious this bond is, and it suffers—they suffer.

Theirs Alone

Perhaps the kind-of-famous singer couple who became famous for being married never considered just what they were doing with those cameras. It probably sounded like an interesting idea that would make them lots of money. But many people ended up under the chuppah with them, and they paid for it.[16]

Because when you give something away, you no longer have it. When a couple shares with others what belongs to the two of them, they pay a price. The power and the mystery and, therefore, the strength of the bond come from the exclusivity. When a couple lets people too far in, when we have experienced what is theirs in some mystical way, they don't have it anymore. They gave it away.

If you do this enough times over a long enough period of time, you'll end up with nothing that's yours and yours alone.

When a couple first gets married, there are a thousand little adjustments they're constantly making, a thousand discussions about the details of life, a thousand conversations about trivial things that are actually significant. On their own, these conversations and interactions don't mean much, but added together, they're how two become one.

What kind of toothpaste do you use? Or do we use the same tube? What side of the bed do you sleep on? Lots of covers, none, a fan, air-conditioning, an open window, an electric blanket, heat turned up or down at night? We're going to a party. Should we bring a gift? How expensive should that gift be? Your parents always took a gift of some sort? Why? Mine never brought a gift—isn't that excessive? What are we going to do? Are we going to follow in the pattern of your family or mine? Or are we going to establish our own way of doing things? A holiday is coming. Your family or mine? Every other holiday with your family? But mine lives close by, yours far away. Why do you keep so many batteries in the refrigerator? Why do you hang your clothes there? I've noticed that when you make your breakfast, you have the strange habit of . . .

And we could go on and on. It's these details, these everyday sorts of lists that sound so minor, that are often at the heart of a marriage. They're what you find out about the person as you begin the lifelong exploration of just who this person is.

A marriage is between those two people, not us. It's not ours, it's theirs.[17]

Especially when it comes to sex.

What goes on between them is a profound mystery. The mystery of the mingling of souls. What goes on under the chuppah belongs to that man and that woman. When it is shared with others, it no longer belongs to them exclusively. And its power is decreased. Because the power of their coming together is rooted in their choice to give themselves to each other and to no one else in this particular way.

Out of six billion people on the planet, I choose you. And no one else. No one else gets this. No one else gets me in this specific, holy, sacred, emotional, spiritual, physical way.

Its power is derived from its exclusivity.

That's why wedding ceremonies stir us like they do. The bride comes down the aisle and gives herself to this man and no one else. They have something with each other that they have with no one else.

We have to be very careful what we share. Because when you give it away, you no longer have it.

The Divine Hovering

The chuppah is a place of confidentiality. If one partner doesn't know whether they can trust the other, they will not share certain things. And these may be the kinds of things that if there were trust, would bring them together.

Is this between you and me,
or you, me, and your friends?

Because that is going to change how much I tell you,
how much I let you in,
how much I trust you with,
how much I give to you.

How naked I get with you.

Is this argument between you and me,
or between you and me and whoever you are going to
tell about it?

Is this quirky habit of mine something I let you see
because I know you love me no matter what, or is this
something you will entertain our friends with at a party?

How safe are you?

There's the profound, mystical sexual union that
happens under the chuppah, with God hovering over
the couple, blessing them. And then there are the
endless conversations and gestures and glances and
discussions as two souls let their lives become
enmeshed in one another.

We live in a world that constantly tries to pull sex out
from under the chuppah.

A culture that shows it,
films it,
examines it,
comments on it,
analyzes it,
and then wonders why everyone has lost interest.

When you take sex out from under the chuppah, all
you are left with is mechanics. Go to any supermarket,
stand in the checkout lane, and count how many of the
women's magazines have the word *technique* somewhere
on the cover. Or the phrase "seven easy steps" or the

word *instructions*. There's nothing wrong with technique and mechanics and instructions, but that's rarely the real issue. The real issue is something else.

The reason people are still watching and discussing and referring to Alfred Hitchcock films is because they're smart and haunting and well done, but most of all because they're scary. But when you watch one, you realize that they're scary in a completely different way than movies that today we would call scary or haunting or creepy are. Hitchcock's genius is that he doesn't show you much at all. He suggests horror and evil without divulging its exact nature, which causes our minds to race ahead and fill in the blanks with what it could be. Our minds are infinitely creative. Given a few well-placed, tactful suggestions, our imaginations kick in and we're scared.

What many modern movies do is show it all, the blood and gore and violence—it all gets shown, we see it, and we may be scared, but it's only for a moment. These movies rarely stay with us because they didn't tap into anything deeper than just the experience of that moment.

Whatever mystery there was, they killed it because they showed everything.

And what's true about things that are scary is true about sex. When sex is taken out from under the chuppah, when it's isolated from its God-intended context, it loses its mystery.

Is God hovering over a couple, making their union holy and sacred?

Some marriage counselors, when they meet with a couple whose marriage is in trouble, immediately take the couple back to when they first met and fell for each other. Counselors and therapists do this because they know that there is some reason why this couple is together. Part of their healing will be rediscovering that initial impulse.

There are six billion people on the planet, and you two ended up together. What was it about him? What was it about her?

Many times people forget their own story—the mystery of what brought them together. How much pain in the world can be tied to people losing the power, the mystery, the holiness of their marriage?

I Always Watch Their Eyes

The creator of the universe has a vested interest in this. God is for marriages.

And it must be protected at all costs, especially in the everyday, subtle sorts of ways. I've been around lots of couples who cut each other down in public, but it's all done in the name of humor.

"The ball and chain . . ."
"My old lady . . ."
"He isn't good for much, but I keep him anyway."

Whenever people talk like this, I always watch their eyes. Is this really all in good fun, or does it carry some truth? Most humor has truth in it.

You can tell when the marriage is in trouble. The jokes have an edge to them. The comments linger just a bit too long on the negative.

And the eyes.
Watch the eyes.

A friend of mine is a doctor who specializes in marriage and relational issues. He says he can tell in a couple of seconds whether a marriage will last. Seriously, a couple of seconds. This is a science called thin slicing, and he's incredibly accurate in his predictions.[18] He says it's all about respect. How he looks at her. How she looks at him. He insists that a few seconds of observing how a couple looks at each other is all he needs to know if the marriage will make it.

Maybe that's another reason why wedding ceremonies are so moving. Watch their eyes. They respect each other. They're under the chuppah.

And then often something happens over time.
The ground becomes less holy.
And they begin to look at each other differently.

Instead of the initial, "Out of all the people in the world, I choose you!" it becomes, "Out of all the people in the world, I chose you?"

Recently I was with a couple who is having serious marriage trouble. I know this, of course, because of how they look at each other. But the wife shares with anyone who will listen just how hard it is to live with her husband. One of their friends was telling me just how toxic the two of them have become to those around them. This friend said that it is so hard because she wants to help, but when the wife tells her things, she has this gut reaction that she shouldn't be hearing them.

This couple needs help. There is trouble under the chuppah. But instead of getting counseling for their issues, they're dragging everything out from under the chuppah and, in the process, making things worse.

A marriage is a sacred, holy thing, and it needs to be treated with respect and honor. They have lost the awareness of just what it is they have, and they're suffering. Actually, lots of people are suffering.

This is why marriage counseling is so powerful. It's two people who are aware of what they have and are willing to protect it and care for it and do whatever it takes to make it better.

Several years ago, I was teaching in our church from the book of Exodus about the chuppah. I had a prayer shawl with me and showed how they would make a canopy out of it and how the bride and groom would stand under it when they exchanged their vows. I got to the end of the teaching and had this sense that something was missing. That I wasn't finished. I then invited people to the stage to stand under the prayer shawl.

People started coming. A married couple would come down, the man obviously being dragged by the woman, but the moment they stood under the chuppah, the man would start crying.

People had strong, emotional responses to simply standing under a sheet.

I met a man the other day who reminded me that it was that moment, five years ago, that changed the whole way he thought about what it meant to give himself to the woman who was his girlfriend at the time, and is now his wife, to love her and devote himself to this sacred, holy thing called marriage. He wanted me to know that it changed his life. Standing under a sheet of fabric for a few moments.

It's just a prayer shawl, right?
A towel on four sticks, correct?
It's a chuppah, but maybe it's more than a chuppah.

CHAPTER EIGHT
JOHNNY AND JUNE

Somebody recently gave me the Johnny Cash *Unearthed* box set.[1] There's around a hundred songs on five CDs, all recorded in the last ten years of Johnny Cash's life. With the box set came a book, and it's fascinating reading. It covers how Johnny Cash's career was revitalized in his later years by producer Rick Rubin, how he would sit for hours at the microphone strumming his guitar and playing the hymns his mother taught him, how he gained a whole new audience of people in their twenties and thirties when he was in his seventies.

But what struck me most were the interviews with the various musicians who consistently mentioned the love between Johnny Cash and his wife, June Carter Cash. What I've come across in everything I've ever read about him or by him is that their love *grew* over the years. They were more in love in their sixties and seventies than ever.

Their marriage got better and better and better.
They were *more* in love as the years went by.

Tom Petty said, "You just couldn't help but love her. John so depended on June, and he so bounced everything off June. It was just such a deep love that it was great to see how the two of them were such a team, really involved in everything together, including the music."

According to Benmont Tench, "She was such a delight . . . He was kind of 'the man in black' and she was this entirely different light, and it was wonderful the way that they fit together."

Here are people in their seventies who have been married for well over thirty years, and the thing that everybody who spent time with them mentions is the love between the two of them.

Whatever it is that they had, it spread.
It spilled over.
It couldn't be contained by just the two of them.
It affected those around them.
It inspired those around them.

Maybe when we meet older couples who obviously still love each other and love being married to each other, we're inspired because so many things around us are in the endless process of falling apart. When something isn't dying but it's going the other way, it's growing. It's not losing life, it's gaining life.

What is it about their marriage that inspires us? Is there something that a couple can do now so that people will talk about them someday like the way they talk about Johnny and June Cash?

To find some answers, we need to go back to the garden of Eden, to God declaring everything "good." The only thing God declares "not good" is Adam's being alone. None of the animals fit with Adam.[2] None of them are adequate to be his partner. After naming them all, he is still lonely. It's in this context that God announces the need for a woman.

There's a mission here. Adam has been commanded to watch over the earth and manage it and creatively order it. Adam has something to do, and it's not good for him to do it alone.

So God says, "I will make a helper suitable for him."[3]

The word *helper* is the word *ezer* in the Hebrew language. We can find it in Psalm 121: "I lift up my eyes to the mountains—where does my help [*ezer*] come from? My help comes from the Lord."[4]

Here it is in Psalm 89, where the words of God are recorded: "I have bestowed strength [*ezer*] on a warrior."[5]

In Psalm 121, the word refers to help that comes from God. In Psalm 89, *ezer* means strength.

To give more depth to the phrase, notice what Adam says about this woman: "This is now bone of my bones and flesh of my flesh."[6] "Bones" is a way of talking about strength, and "flesh" is a way of talking about weakness. He's essentially saying, "Where I am weak, she is strong, and where she is weak, I am strong."

Eve is a corresponding strength for Adam.
They fit together.
They fill each other in.
They cover for each other.
They're better off together than apart.

The passage continues: "For this reason a man will leave his father and mother and be united to his wife."[7]

This leaving involves his whole life. This leaving involves her whole life. They cannot do this halfheartedly. They have to commit all the way. They have to give everything to it. His place of residence and his primary ties to his parents and family now take second place to his commitment to her.

A new family has formed.

Echad

Think of how many marriages suffer because one or both of the people maintain all sorts of ties and connections with their family of origin that get in the way of their new marriage bond. Their first loyalty is now to each other, not to their families. Obviously this is not about cutting off contact with your parents or having nothing to do with them, at least in most cases. It's about realizing just how profound this uniting is.[8]

So the man leaves his parents, unites with the woman, "and they will become one flesh."[9]

Now the one flesh seems to be about their having sex. Which, of course, it is. But there is so much more going on here. Even having sex in this story is about something else.

In the Jewish consciousness, words are extremely meaningful. While an English dictionary has somewhere between one and two hundred thousand words, the Hebrew language has around seven thousand words.[10]

So in Hebrew, words have to cover a lot of ground. A single word can have tremendous depth and significance. When it is said that the man and woman will become "one flesh," the word for *one* in Hebrew is the word *echad*.

Echad is oneness made up of several parts or members.[11] So the man and woman are two people, two separate, independent beings, and yet when they come together, they're "one." The word is significant because it occurs in one of the most well-known passages of scripture in Jewish history. It's a prayer from the book of Deuteronomy that begins, "Hear, O Israel: The Lord our God, the Lord is one."[12]

This prayer, called the *Shema,* from the word "to hear," is the central declaration of the Jewish faith, a way of reaffirming all that life is about. It's said by Jews when they wake up, when they go to sleep, when they gather on the Sabbath, when they study, when someone dies— there are numerous legends of great Jews having it on their lips as they were martyred.

The Lord is one.
The Lord is *echad.*
God is *echad.*

It's the same word as the "one flesh" in Genesis: "And the man and woman shall be *echad* flesh."

Central to the Bible is the affirmation that there is one God. Not many, one. And sex between the man and woman has something to do with God.

Who God is.
What God is like.
Adam and Eve are one as God is one.
Same word.

This marriage between a man and woman—their having sex—is about something much bigger than the relationship itself. It points beyond them to somebody else—to God.

The point of marriage isn't marriage.
It's a picture.
A display.

A window that you look through to something else.
A marriage has a mission.

Our world isn't *echad*. It isn't one. It's broken, shattered,
fractured, with pieces lying all over the floor.

We all have friends who are from "broken homes."
A couple "split up."
A spouse is "shattered" by his lover's infidelity.
Somebody's marriage fell apart and she's "picking up the
pieces."

When our trust has been betrayed and those who
were supposed to stand by us don't, this naturally has
consequences for how we think about God. It becomes
hard to trust that God is good when our significant
relationships simply aren't that good.

A marriage is designed to counter all of this. Not to
add to the brokenness of the world but to add to the
"oneness" of the world. This man and this woman who
have given themselves to each other are supposed to
give the world a glimpse of hope, a display of what
God is like, a bit of *echad* on earth.

They Thrive, We Thrive

Is that where the phrase "making love" comes from? An
awareness that something mystical happens in sex, that
something good and needed is created?[13] Something is
added to the world, given to the world. The world is

blessed with something that it desperately needs. This man and this woman together are in some profoundly mysterious way good for the well-being of the whole world.

When we go to a wedding, maybe we're so moved because we want this new couple to succeed. We intuitively know that their "success" is somehow tied to ours. Their making of love makes the world a better place to live, a place where there is more love for all of us. Maybe this is why we always notice great marriages. When their love is growing, it inspires us. Their life together gives *us* life.

A wedding reminds us that it's all connected.
We're all connected.

So when it's written that Adam and Eve were one flesh, their "*echad* flesh" is actually a celebration of a million other things. Things that ought to be celebrated: God. Life. Creativity. Potential. Shared partnership in caring for the world. Strength for weakness, weakness for strength. A new family. The ongoing creation of the world.

And finally, after all of this leaving and cleaving and bones and flesh, the passage ends with the line "the man and his wife were both naked, and they felt no shame."[14]

No shame or embarrassment.
No apologizing for who they are.
No covering up or pretending.
No masks or secrets.

Total acceptance of each other.
That's what we want, isn't it?

We want someone to see us exactly as we are and still love us.

It's terrifying to let people see who we really are. To see the darkness in our hearts, our bad habits, all of the things we've done in the past that we regret. Our biases, our shortcomings, the things we aren't good at.

Being naked is terrifying.

What would it be like to be with someone who loves you exactly as you are?

If you see me for who I really am, the me that no one else has ever seen, the me that I wouldn't dare to show anybody else on the planet, the parts of me I'm not sure I want anybody ever to see, if I give you that kind of glimpse into the seat of my being, into my soul, will you still love me like you do now?

It's our question for each other, and it's our question for God.

Unconditional, absolute acceptance.
From a lover, from God—it's what we crave.

This is why a marriage is always about something bigger than itself. It's two people, in their unconditionally loving embrace of each other, showing each other in flesh and blood what God is like. These two are naked, and they feel no shame.

Out of Order

There's a progression here, a pattern in this passage for how we're made to connect with another. It's built into the fabric of creation. There's a way for souls to mingle.

And it's possible to get this progression out of order. We have to understand that we were created by God to live as integrated beings. Whole. One. Not splintered and fractured but one.

In the Psalms, it's written that "fools say in their hearts . . ." It's written in another psalm, "My spirit asked . . ." In another, "My heart and my flesh cry out . . ."[15] Hearts speak and spirits ask and flesh cries out. The body and the soul and the brain and the heart and thoughts and feelings are all merged into one being we call a person.

The passage in Genesis about Adam and Eve is about whole persons coming together. All of him being given to all of her. All of her being given to all of him.

If he wants her just for her body, that splits her. It means that she is good to him only for a part of her. That's why when she's slept with him, she wants to know where the relationship is headed. She wants to be integrated. She craves it. She wants to know that he will be there in the morning, and the next morning, and the next morning. She wants to know that beyond the sex, he loves her, he wants her—all of her.

The "naked and they felt no shame" part comes last in the story of Adam and Eve. It's a celebration of all of the ways they've bonded. All of the ways their souls have mingled.

It's easy to take off your clothes and have sex. People do it all the time. But opening up your soul to someone, letting them into your spirit

and thoughts
and fears
and future
and hopes
and dreams . . .
that is being naked.

This is why when people sleep together after they've just met, they're raising the chances significantly that the relationship will not survive. Racing ahead of the progression always costs something.

When there is no common mission, no shared task, no sense of bone of bone and flesh of flesh, no bonds that take years to develop, many end up moving from relationship to relationship, having sex but never really being naked.

Too much too fast rarely endures.

As it says in the Song of Songs, "Do not arouse or awaken love until it so desires."[16]

I have some friends who have been married over thirty years. They have one of those Johnny and June marriages. I was in a meeting with them last week, and I noticed that when the meeting was over and everybody was leaving the room, they were still seated, deep in conversation about something. He was smiling. She was leaning close to him as she spoke. It reminded me of a conversation I'd had with him recently in which he was telling me about a vacation they'd just taken and how the highlight for him was the conversations he had with his wife.

It struck me as I walked out of the room: they're still getting to know each other. Still talking, still telling stories, still exploring just who this person is. They understand that people are highly complex beings and that the soul is infinitely deep. If you're mingling your soul with another soul, and there's no end to the depth of both of your souls, this could take a while.[17]

Which reminds me of an outdoor restaurant I ate at last week. At the table next to ours was a couple, probably in their early fifties. I noticed as we walked in that they weren't talking. Which isn't that unusual. But I watched them again after we'd sat down and ordered. And they still weren't talking. And so I must be honest and say that I began checking on them every minute or so.

And they just sat there.

I assume you've seen this before. Couples who don't talk. I'm fully aware that you can have an off night and that sometimes sitting in silence together can be very peaceful. But some couples, though they're together, they're a million miles apart.

Infinite Depth

To pursue being naked, you have to believe that this person is worth getting to know for the rest of your lives. Being naked is peeling back the layers, conversation after conversation, experience after experience, year after year. It's rooted in a belief that the soul has infinite depth and you'll never get to the bottom of it.[18]

Our understanding of what it means to be naked reflects what we believe about the human soul. Is it infinite? Or can you get to the end of a person?

The failure to understand the infinite depth of the human soul is often why people who are married have affairs. They stop exploring the person they married. They find somebody who appears more interesting.

Another couple I've known for a while just told me that they have been taking dancing lessons. They've been married well over thirty-five years, and they've just taken up a hobby together that's new to both of them. It's so simple, taking up a hobby together, and yet it's so profound.

CHAPTER NINE

WHOOPEE FOREVER

Sometimes when I hear someone talking about the "Christian ideal" for sex and marriage, I laugh.

Jesus says in Matthew, "For some are eunuchs because they were born that way; others have been made eunuchs; and others have renounced marriage because of the kingdom of heaven. The one who can accept this should accept it."[1]

According to Jesus, some people are so devoted to God that they don't need to be married. They have transcended the married state, moving past it to a place of union with God in which having a spouse is simply unnecessary. Now, obviously if everybody did this, we would have no future anybodies, but the point is, Jesus states this matter-of-factly. As if it's the most normal thing imaginable.

So according to Jesus, there's being married, and then there's something else.

In the book of Luke, Jesus says, "The people of this age marry and are given in marriage. But those who are considered worthy of taking part in the age to come and in the resurrection from the dead will neither marry nor be given in marriage, and they can no longer die; for they are like the angels."[2]

In the first text, Jesus claims that some have "renounced marriage" for a state of union with God. But in the second text, he says that this will be true for all sorts of people in "the age to come," the implication being that this will be true for people who are married now.

And in Matthew 19, Jesus affirms the one man, one woman marriage bond, the "one flesh" of Genesis, adding, "Therefore what God has joined together, let no one separate."[3]

So Jesus has no problem with marriage and sex. He goes to weddings and quotes Genesis and celebrates all that should be celebrated. It's just that he sees marriage, and therefore sex, as not the ultimate state.

Maybe the better word here is *temporary*. Sex, marriage, husbands, and wives—all appear to Jesus to be quite temporary, not in this life but in the next one, the one after this.

With Jesus's words in mind, notice the words of Paul in First Corinthians: "I wish that all of you were as I am." Paul wasn't married, so he's telling his audience that he wishes they were unmarried as he was. "But each of you has your own gift from God; one has this gift, another has that. Now to the unmarried and the widows I say: It is good for them to stay unmarried, as I do. But if they cannot control themselves, they should marry, for it is better to marry than to burn with passion."[4]

That's a great line, isn't it? "Better to marry than to burn"—a classic.

Paul continues, "Now about virgins: I have no command from the Lord, but I give a judgment as one who by the Lord's mercy is trustworthy. Because of the present crisis, I think that it is good for a man to remain as he is. Are you pledged to a woman? Do not seek to be released. Are you free from such a commitment? Do not look for a wife. But if you do marry, you have not sinned; and if a virgin marries, she has not sinned."[5]

If you're married, you haven't sinned.
Well, that's a relief.

But he's not done: "But those who marry will face many troubles in this life, and I want to spare you this. . . . I would like you to be free from concern. An unmarried man is concerned about the Lord's affairs—how he can please the Lord. But a married man is concerned about the affairs of this world—how he can please his wife—and his interests are divided. . . . A woman is bound to her husband as long as he lives. But if her husband dies, she is free to marry anyone she wishes, but he must belong to the Lord. In my judgment, she is happier if she stays as she is—and I think that I too have the Spirit of God."[6]

Paul doesn't seem concerned about whether a person is married. If you aren't, great. You're more free to serve God. If you are married, splendid. Love the person well, and the two of you get on with your life together.

After all, it's better to marry than to burn.

Missing Something?

Paul says that he doesn't have some sort of black-and-white message from God on whether people should be married. It's possible for destructive messages to be sent to people who are single. That they are second class, less than, that they don't fit, that they should find someone, get married, and join the rest of us who are "normal."

If you are single, and you've been sent messages or it's been hinted at or even said to your face that you are somehow missing something, that you aren't good enough, that you don't fit—that is not true. It's not just that you're fine single. The premise of the scriptures is that you are able to connect with God and serve God in ways that those who are married can't. The tilt is *for* being single, not away from it.

The last thing Jesus ever says, or even implies, is that people who aren't married are somehow missing out. So according to Jesus, if you aren't having sex, you aren't missing out on anything. And if you aren't missing out, and marriage, according to the scriptures, is somehow temporary, then what does this say about our future?

Our future, together, after this life?
What does sex now say about life forever?

A good place to start is the end. The Bible ends with a book called Revelation, written by a man named John. In the last two chapters, John paints a picture of "a new heaven and a new earth," which he says will come about at some point in the future. He looks and sees "the Holy City, the new Jerusalem, coming down out of heaven from God, prepared as a bride beautifully dressed for her husband."[7]

Of all of the symbols and metaphors and images he has to draw from, John describes the end of the world as we know it as a wedding celebration. For John's Jewish audience, this made perfect sense. This goes all the way back to the Exodus and Mount Sinai. To God and God's people, coming together at the mountain. To the Shekinah hovering over them. To the marriage of the divine and the human.

To God's desire to be with people.

The text continues: "And I heard a loud voice from the throne saying, 'Look! God's dwelling place is now among the people, and he will dwell with them.' "[8]

God with Us

The vision John has is not of people leaving earth and going somewhere else. It's a vision of God coming here and taking up residence in our midst.

What would *that* be like? We read that this city "does not need the sun or the moon to shine on it, for the glory of God gives it light."[9]

Light exposes things. Light shows how things really are. There is no hiding in the light. Light is freedom. There is nothing to fear because everything is shown to be exactly what it is.

In the light, everybody is known fully.

Which is what people crave in sex, isn't it? To be known fully and still loved, still embraced, still accepted.

We read that in this city, "nothing impure will ever enter it."[10] Isn't that what sex is supposed to be for people in its greatest moment? When it is free from power and coercion and manipulation and agendas and fears, when it is simply two people giving all of themselves to each other, holding nothing back?

We read in John's account that there is a tree of life in this city, and that "the leaves of the tree are for the healing of the nations."[11] The healing of the nations is the dream of the Jewish prophets, the dream of God—for everybody to finally get along. No war, no conflict, no strife. Harmony between all of humanity. Isn't that the dream of any relationship? Isn't that why people continue to step into relationships, even when they've been hurt time and time again? Because we still find new ways to hope that there, we will finally get along with somebody.

All of us connected with each other in one giant global embrace.

We read that in this city, "no longer will there be any curse."[12] The curse is a reference to the entrance of death into the human story in the garden of Eden. This curse is everywhere we look. Even the best possible relationships have a certain ache to them because someday, inevitably, one person is going to stand over the casket of the other. It all ends there. For everyone.

For many people, sex is brief moments when everything is okay with the world, even if it isn't. It's escape from the pain and suffering and brokenness of life. It's a short time when all is right, even if lots of things around us are falling apart.

In Revelation, God announces, "I am making everything new!"[13] Isn't that the longing of every embrace, every act of love, sex itself? To start again, to give yourself away, again, to try again for hope and healing and restoration?

We find sex so powerful because it provides people with glimpses into the world we all desperately desire but can't seem to create on our own.

Which raises a few questions.

If marriage has a purpose, to bring hope to the world, what happens when the world doesn't need hope?

What happens to marriage when every hope has been fulfilled?

If sex is about connection, what happens when everybody is connected with everybody else?

If marriage is about the man and the woman filling each other in, complementing each other, bone of bones and flesh of flesh, what happens when the man and woman are complete in and of themselves?

What happens when everything we need from each other we have in God?

What happens in the presence of God when we are everything we were originally created to be?

If marriage is meant to show people what the oneness of God is like, what happens when everybody is one in the presence of God?[14]

If marriage is a picture of something else, what would happen to marriage if we found ourselves living in the midst of that something else?

Is sex in its greatest, purest, most joyful and honest expression a glimpse of forever?

Are these brief moments of abandon and oneness and ecstasy just a couple of seconds or minutes of how things will be forever?

Is sex a picture of heaven?

In First Corinthians 12, Paul claimed to have seen a vision of heaven, and the phrase he used to describe it in Greek is translated "unwordable words." He wrote that he saw things man is "not permitted to tell."

Maybe that's why the scriptures are so ambivalent about whether a person is married. About whether a person is having sex.

Maybe Jesus knew what is coming and knew that whatever we experience here will pale compared with what awaits everyone.

Do you long for that?
Because that's the center of Jesus's message.
An invitation.
To trust that it's true,
to trust that it's real,
to trust that God is actually going to make all things new.

My Father's House

In the first century, generally a young woman would be married in her early teens, often at thirteen or fourteen. It would become known that she was now "of age," and her father would entertain offers from the fathers of young men who were interested in marrying her. If the fathers agreed on the terms of the marriage, there would be a celebration to honor the couple and announce their engagement. At this celebration, the groom would offer the young girl a cup of wine to drink.[15]

But she doesn't have to drink it.

She can reject the cup. She can say no to his offer of marriage. Even though everything has already been arranged, she can still say no. It's up to her.

Can you imagine the pressure on the young fella?

Here is everybody you love the most, friends and parents and relatives, gathered in a room, watching to see if she will accept the cup.

If she says yes, the groom gives a sort of prepared speech about their future together.

Because if she takes the cup and drinks from it, that only means that they are engaged. They aren't married yet. Something still has to happen.

Or to be more precise, something has to be built.

If she says yes, then the groom goes home and begins building an addition onto his family's home. This is where he and his bride will start their new family together. And so he works and works and works, building a place that they can call home. And here's the interesting part: he doesn't know when he's going to finish. Because he doesn't have the final say on whether it's ready. That's his father's decision. And so his father periodically inspects his work, looking to see if the quality of what the son is building properly honors his future bride. The father has considerations as well. If he has many sons, and they've all built additions, then his house is getting quite large. There are many rooms in it. This was called an *insula,* a large multifamily dwelling. If the father had built his addition onto his father's house, then by now, several generations later, this is a large dwelling with rooms for a lot of people.

Back to the story.

The future bride is at home, learning how to run a household. She also doesn't know when the work will be done, so she's preparing herself for a date that's coming, she just doesn't know when.

And then the day comes. The father inspects and tells the son that it's time. So the son gets his friends, and they set out for her house to get her. But how will he know what room is hers?

He'll know because she has filled her lamp with oil each night and set it in the window, so that when he comes, he'll know which room is hers.[16]

And so he goes to get her, and they gather their friends and family, and there's a giant procession back to his house, where the party starts.

And so when she takes the glass of wine at their engagement party and drinks from it, the groom says to her: "My father's house has plenty of room; if that were not so, would I have told you that I am going there to prepare a place for you? And if I go and prepare a place for you, I will come back and take you to be with me that you also may be where I am. You know the way to the place where I am going."

Does his speech sound familiar? This is what Jesus says to his disciples in John 14:2–4.

When Jesus wants to assure his followers that they're going to be okay, that their future is secure, that they shouldn't let their hearts be troubled, he uses the wedding metaphor.

They would have known exactly what he was talking about. They would have heard the groom's speech growing up, the ones who were married would have given it to their brides, and they all would have taken part in numerous wedding celebrations.

To describe heaven, Jesus uses an event they had all experienced and basically says, "It's like that."

That is like this?

MORE BALLOONS, PLEASE

A book like this can go two ways.

For some, hopefully, light has been shed on things that matter. "Oh, that finally makes sense," or, "I never thought about it like that," or even, "Huh . . . I'll have to think about that."

But for others, all this subject does is bring up pain and regret. Relationships, mistakes, the endless breaking of the heart. All of the ways we've missed out on how things were meant to be. Perhaps this book has opened wounds you thought were healed years ago.

Several years ago, I conducted a wedding ceremony on a Saturday afternoon in June. The bride wore a white summer dress, the groom a white linen shirt. They insisted on the simplest ceremony possible. It was held in a park in a grove of trees. Their family and friends stood in a circle, with the three of us in the middle. I began with a welcome, they exchanged vows and rings, I pronounced them husband and wife, they kissed, everybody clapped. The ceremony took seven minutes.

They were then each handed a cluster of helium balloons on strings. The balloons, I told everybody, were symbols of their past marriages, pregnancies they had chosen to terminate, people they had had affairs with when they were previously married, relationships that had not lasted. As a picture of starting over, together, they wanted their first act as a married couple to be letting the balloons go.

They walked out of the grove of trees into an adjoining field. Just the two of them, holding hands, standing in knee-high grass, exchanging words that only they could hear. Then they raised the balloons above their heads and let them go. We all stood there, watching those balloons float away until they drifted from sight.

There are moments you wonder if you'll ever forget. Events that sear themselves on your conscience. That moment was one of those for me.

A few years later their marriage imploded. She moved an hour away. He relocated to another part of the country. They divorced.

I finish with this story because life is messy. Gut wrenching. Risky. Things don't always turn out well. Sometimes they don't turn out at all. Sometimes everything falls apart and we wonder if there's any point to any of it. We're tempted to shut ourselves off, fortify the walls around our hearts, and forge ahead, promising ourselves that we will never open ourselves up like that again.

But I have to believe that we can recover from anything. I have to believe that God can put anything—anyone—back together. I have to believe that the God Jesus invites us to trust is as good as he says he is.

Loving.
Forgiving.
Merciful.
Full of grace.

And I have to believe that God does not run out of balloons.

ENDNOTES

INTRODUCTION **THIS IS REALLY ABOUT THAT**

1 Genesis 25, 27.

2 Genesis 28:11. "In a certain place" is one of the many places in the Bible where phrases and words appear to be ordinary and yet are the windows and doors to new understandings of the story.

3 Verse 15. There is a vast tradition of commentary on this passage. Lawrence Kushner's *God Was in This Place and I, I Did Not Know It* (Jewish Lights Publishers) is an excellent place to start. Read this book with your friends and you'll have things to talk about for years.

4 For examples of this, see 1 Kings 3:2; 11:7; 12:31; 13:2; 14:23; and 22:43.

5 Verses 20–21.

6 Genesis 35:7.

7 I'm sure Jacob's kids understood altars and shrines and piles of rocks in the sense that people did this all the time in the ancient Near East. My hypothetical dialogue between Jacob and his children is about why. Why this altar here, Dad? The most symbolic act here would have been the standing of one stone, called a *massabah* in Hebrew, on top of all the others.

CHAPTER ONE **GOD WEARS LIPSTICK**

1 I first came across Gonin's diary in the manifesto of the legendary British graffiti artist named Banksy, whom you must get to know (Banksy.co.uk). He cites the Imperial War Museum as his source for the diary (Banksy, *Wall and Piece*).

2 Genesis 1:27.

3 Several excellent commentaries on Genesis: Nahum Sarrna's *Understanding Genesis,* Henri Blocher's *In the Beginning,* and *JPS Torah Commentary,* Genesis edition.

4 *JPS Torah Commentary:* "While he is not divine, his very existence bears witness to the activity of God in the life of the world" (12).

5 I used the phrase "divine spark." What would you call it? When have you seen it? How do you describe it?

6 Recently I saw my friend Josh, who teaches fifth and sixth graders. He was preparing the lesson for that day and had his supplies with him: a large glass bowl, a can of beef, fatty tissue, sauerkraut, a jar of olives, some anchovies, and a hundred-dollar bill. I know— I was curious too. So I did exactly what you would have done. I asked him what his lesson was about. He replied, "I put all of the ingredients in a bowl, including the money, and then I mix it together. Then when it doesn't taste good, I pretend I'm going to throw it away. At this point the kids go crazy, telling me not to. I ask them why I shouldn't, and they say, 'Because it's valuable.' And then I counter with, 'But it smells and it's disgusting.' At which point they rush to the front, volunteering to reach into the bowl and pull out the hundred-dollar bill. Actually, I may have to start using a twenty for this lesson, because the last time I used a

hundred, they trampled each other to get to the front. I then read to them from Genesis chapter 1 about how every single human being bears the image of God and how no matter what else is mixed in there, a person still has limitless worth in God's eyes."

7 Does this sound familiar? Does this stop when you leave high school? Have you ever been that girl? Or that boy? Or that crowd?

8 Matthew 5:27–30.

9 Which makes sense if you've ever had someone angry with you. It doesn't matter whether they've acted on that anger, just the fact that you know they're angry with you means *something*. Something that is in their heart and is never expressed still hurts. Why is this?

10 What book would be complete without at least one Monty Python reference?

11 Psalm 103:19.

12 Psalm 115:16.

13 For a very helpful explanation of hell, read chapter 10 in *Following Jesus* by N. T. Wright.

14 In Matthew 18:6, Jesus uses the image of a millstone being hung around someone's neck before they're thrown into the sea. In Luke 19:11–27, in the parable of the ten minas, the story he tells ends with the delegation being slaughtered in front of the king. And in Luke 20:9–19, the heir is killed, and in response the owner kills the tenants. Why does Jesus tell so many stories and use so many examples that involve violence?

15 The organization my friend worked with is called International Justice Mission (IJM.org). Give them lots of money so that they can continue to do great things among the most forgotten and oppressed. Freetheslaves.net reports that there are 27 million slaves in the world . . . today. More than ever in human history.

16 Ephesians 2.

17 Genesis 1–11.

18 The word *community* comes from the word *common.* Community isn't really created—it's discovered. We discover what we've had in common all along. We don't make these bonds from scratch, we merely become aware of bonds that have been there all along.

19 Exodus 12; Matthew 26; 1 Corinthians 11.

20 Matthew 22:39, which is from Leviticus 19:18.

21 Lil's husband's name is Warren, and you really must meet him sometime.

22 Jean Vanier's *Becoming Human* is a classic work on seeing "only one label."

CHAPTER TWO **SEXY ON THE INSIDE**

1 For a powerful look at how life in the modern world is affecting how we spend our time, read *In Praise of Slow* by Carl Honoré.

2 Two of the best books I have read on our relationship to the earth are *For the Beauty of the Earth* by Steven Bouma-Prediger and Barbara Kingsolver's *Small Wonder.* And then, when you're done with those two books, you really must get your hands on Kingsolver's stunning piece of literature called *The Poisonwood Bible.*

3 Genesis 1–3.

4 Several of the big ideas in this chapter were inspired and affirmed and guided by Ronald Rolheiser's *The Holy Longing.* I cannot recommend this book highly enough.

5 Ephesians 4:6.

6 Hebrews 2:10.

7 Marva Dawn makes this distinction in her magnificent book *Sexual Character.*

8 Rolheiser puts it this way: "We are built to ultimately embrace the universe and everything in it."

9 I call him a friend, but he's a hero and a prophet as well. Shane Claiborne lives in Philadelphia and recently wrote a book called *Irresistible Revolution.*

10 As one said recently, "I can't imagine being married. It would take so much time!"

11 One of the best books on learning how to forgive people I've come across is Lewis Smedes's *Art of Forgiving.*

12 Trust me, she's that brilliant quite often. She insists that she got this from an interview with Bono in which he used the phrase. I say we credit them both.

CHAPTER THREE **ANGELS AND ANIMALS**

1 There's an advertising campaign running right now for the city of Las Vegas that says, "Whatever happens in Las Vegas, stays in Las Vegas." How boring does your life have to be that you need to go somewhere far away and do things you don't want anybody to know about to have a good time?

2 1 Corinthians 6:13.

3 1 Corinthians 6:19. He's writing to a church here, a group of people, so the "you" is plural.

4 Blaise Pascal said, "Man is neither angel nor beast" (*Pensées* [London: Dent, 1960], 68).

5 I'm using the word *spirit* here in reference to the distinction made in Genesis between humans and the rest of creation, humans being made in the image of God. In the sense that the word for spirit is also the word for *breath* in both Hebrew and Greek, then obviously animals do have spirits, as we read in Ecclesiastes 3:21.

6 Job 38:7.

7 Psalm 8:5.

8 Hebrews 1:14.

9 Being fully human is our job. Thinking and laughing and arranging and creating and relating and designing and nurturing and responding and reacting and pondering when googling became a verb and wondering and exploring and meditating and acting and making long lists of verbs and calling and talking and feeling and sharing and doubting if this paragraph is ever going to end and teaching and learning and jumping on a trampoline and sighing and celebrating and dancing and turning to the person next to you and saying: "This is living."

You can make your own list because you know what it is that makes you feel alive, what it is that feeds your soul, what it is that reminds you that the goal is to be fully human. What's on your list?

I've heard people say, "I'm only human," as if it's a bad thing. But being human isn't a bad thing; it's a good thing. It's what God intended. How could we ever be anything else?

The issue, then, isn't trying to escape our humanity in order to morph into something, or somebody, else. The problem is all of the things that get in the way of being fully human. When a person says, "I'm only human," perhaps what they mean is, "I have this habit of making choices that inhibit my being fully human." This is a primal struggle in all of us, and it goes all the way back to the garden of Eden. The temptation was, and is, to trade our full humanity for something else.

10 1 Timothy 4:1–5.

11 1 Timothy 4:3.

12 Verses 4–5.

13 *The God Factor* by Cathleen Falsani.

14 The word *confession* in the Hebrew language literally means "to cast or throw out." To confess simply means to get it out.

15 xxxchurch.com, a resource for porn-addiction recovery.

16 I was on vacation with my extended family, miles from pavement and the internet and the phone and the news, when my sister-in-law joined us, having flown across the country to get there. After she had unpacked and gotten settled, she came into the living room and said to me, "I thought you'd enjoy these. I bought them in the airport."

As she said this, she placed in front of me a stack of *those* magazines. You know the ones I'm talking about—the glossy ones with pictures of celebrities doing extraordinary things like getting coffee and picking something up at the dry cleaners and walking their dogs. *Those* magazines, the ones that you tell yourself you're not going to read because it's meaningless fluff and yet you find yourself getting your oil changed or at the dentist's office or waiting to get your hair cut . . . and you're hooked.

It seems that while I had been away in the woods something very important was happening with a famous handsome actor that we all needed to know about. He was filming a movie with a famous actress, and rumors had started that their relationship was more than professional. They denied it and he proved they were just rumors by appearing in public with his beautiful actress wife, whom everybody loves. But then he and his wife announced they were separating. And then came the shocker: pictures of the famous handsome actor on vacation with the famous actress he was in the movie with. Reading this story in the magazine my sister-in-law put in front of me, I had only one question: "Do the other magazines have any important details this magazine missed?" And so I read and read until I was fully abreast of the situation.

Because, of course, we all need to know.

What struck me most was what the famous actress said about their affair, which was now public thanks to the covers of a multitude of magazines. She said that she and the famous handsome actor "couldn't help themselves."

Couldn't help themselves?

Now these are incredibly disciplined people who are known for their outstanding work ethic. If they want to gain weight or lose weight or learn an accent or acquire a new skill for a film, they do it. They're both legendary for how much—let me find the right word here—for how much control they're able to exercise over their lives. They've built incredibly successful careers on it. And yet when it comes to each other—when it comes to sex—they "can't help themselves."

Why is this? Is it just the way it is? Can you relate?

17 Genesis 1.

CHAPTER FOUR **LEATHER, WHIPS, AND FRUIT**

1 2 Samuel 13:1–22.

2 Renée Altson's *Stumbling toward Faith* is an honest, raw, hopeful memoir by someone who's healing from sexual abuse. The first page of the first chapter will take your breath away.

3 Genesis 1–3.

4 Genesis 3:6. It was a watermelon.

5 For a very insightful look at the philosophy of design, read John Maeda's *The Laws of Simplicity*.

6 Ephesians 4:18.

7 The last reflections of Anthony Demello, *The Way to Love.*

8 Look up the word remember in a concordance of the Bible. Why does it occur so often?

9 1 Corinthians 6:12.

10 Ephesians 4:18.

11 Ephesians 4:19.

12 Ephesians 6:19.

13 Garrett Keizer writes in his book *The Enigma of Anger* that the worldview of the lustful "runs counter to God's vision. Nothing they see is good, or good enough, or else nothing they see is enough of the good. In other words, you can never please them, which is as good a definition as you may get of what it means to be damned."

14 Cornelius Plantinga in his book *Engaging God's World* has a brilliant quote about the devil wearing makeup. Essentially, that which isn't good has to dress up and disguise itself as good to get our attention.

15 Ephesians 4:28.

16 In the book of Luke, in chapter 9, we're told that Jesus "resolutely set out for Jerusalem."

Then in chapter 13 we're told that Jesus was going through the towns and villages, "teaching as he made his way to Jerusalem."

In chapter 17 we read, "Now on his way to Jerusalem . . ."

And then chapter 18, "Jesus took the Twelve aside and told them, 'We are going up to Jerusalem.'"

And then in chapter 19, "After Jesus had said this, he went on ahead, going up to Jerusalem."

Apparently Luke wants us to see something here, and so he brings it up again and again and again. Jesus is going to—let's all say it together—Jerusalem.

Jesus has given his life to something. And this something that he's given his life to is taking him to Jerusalem, to a confrontation with the religious establishment. He's given his energies to this—to healing, to teaching, and to identifying with the outcasts and the unclean along the way. He's on the way somewhere. There's even a point where he's been in a village and he's leaving and the people of the village try to get him to stay. But he leaves anyway. He is able to walk away from people who are pleading with him to stay in their village. How can he walk away?

Because he has a larger calling he's given himself to: going to Jerusalem.

CHAPTER FIVE SHE RAN INTO THE GIRLS' BATHROOM

1 Song of Songs 2:8-13.

2 5:2-6.

3 This is a joke.

4 No offense to country music fans everywhere.

5 This is called anthropomorphism, giving God human attributes. God is spirit, without gender or form or shape or physicality, so when we say that God "has a heart," it's a metaphor, a figure of speech, a way of explaining things in language we can understand.

6 Please go read everything Donald Miller has ever written.

7 Yes, I'm referring to *Star Wars*. May the force be with you.

8 Exodus 20:1-21.

9 Verse 18-19. Later, in Exodus 34, Moses has to wear a veil because

he's been on the mountain with God and when he returns to the people, again they can't handle it. "And they were afraid to come near him."

10 Matthew 1:18–24.

11 Luke 2:7.

12 Mark 3:21.

13 Luke 4:14–30.

14 Matthew 8:1–4.

15 Luke 7:36–50.

16 Luke 7:14. Actually, the text says he touches the bier they were carrying the dead man on, which we would assume includes touching the dead man.

17 John 4:1–42.

18 Matthew 21:1–11.

19 Luke 19:41.

20 Matthew 16:21; Mark 8:31; 9:12; Luke 9:22; 17:25; 22:15. Notice how late in the story he mentions that he's going to suffer, but once he first mentions it, he then starts mentioning it more and more often.

21 Luke 23:8.

22 John 19:28.

23 The statements Jesus makes on the cross are quotes from Psalm 22. It makes for a fascinating study, especially in light of how Psalm 22 ends.

24 Philippians 2:5–11.

25 Matthew 5.

26 I just bought a book by Mark Kurlansky called *Nonviolence:*

Twenty-five Lessons from the History of a Dangerous Idea. This is a book we need to be reading now more than ever.

27 Luke 23:47.

28 If you are that girl who wouldn't dance with me, I have forgiven you.

CHAPTER SIX **WORTH DYING FOR**

1 For an in-depth, accessible explanation of this passage, see John Bristow's *What Paul Really Said about Women*.

The verb *submit* here is in the imperative, middle voice. The active voice means you are doing it, the passive voice is when it's being done to you, and the middle voice is a voluntary action by the subject on the subject, such as teaching yourself. It's something you do to yourself voluntarily, willingly, actively.

2 John 3:16.

3 John 15:13.

4 Song of Songs 6:3.

5 1 Corinthians 7:3–4.

6 1 Corinthians 4:21; John 15:13; Romans 13:10; 1 John 4:7; Ephesians 2:4.

7 Frederick Buechner's *Secrets in the Dark* has a section on agape that is stunning. A classic book on agape is C. S. Lewis's *The Four Loves*.

8 Romans 5:8.

9 1 Corinthians 1:26.

10 Jeremiah 1:4–5.

11 John 15:16.

12 Theologians call this "escatalogical realism."

13 When Jesus is tempted in the wilderness (Matt. 4), the tempter begins, "If you are the Son of God . . ." And yet several verses earlier, at Jesus's baptism, the voice from heaven had just declared, "This is my Son, whom I love, with him I am well pleased."

14 There's a poem in the Bible called the Song of Songs, in which the woman says that she wants the man to "kiss me with the kisses of his mouth—for your love is more delightful than wine" (1:2). She tells him, "Take me away with you" (1:4). She says she's "faint with love" (2:5).

She is sexually alive, full of longing, expressing herself, full of desire—this is a woman with no hangups. And yet she says something fascinating later on in the poem. She says, "But my own vineyard is mine to give" (8:12).

Why is this significant? Because in the ancient Near East, a vineyard is a metaphor for sexuality. She's not going to give herself away to just anybody. It's her decision, and she will make it without coercion or manipulation.

She's alive sexually, and yet it doesn't control her.

And how does the man respond?

He tells her, "You are a garden locked up . . . you are a spring enclosed, a sealed fountain" (4:12). "You are a garden fountain, a well of flowing water" (4:15).

Why all of this talk about water? Because it's a symbol of life and vitality and energy and purity. He's praising her for her control of her sexuality. He isn't pressuring her, piling on the guilt because she's so tight, making her feel like she's repressed. He's thrilled that she doesn't give herself to just anyone.

So here are these two people who are totally alive sexually and who can talk about it, who can express themselves to each other openly and honestly, and yet they aren't at the mercy of their urges. They're able to live on some higher plane. There is something guiding them that's deeper and stronger than just their sexual urges.

15 Every woman should read Wendy Shalit's *Return to Modesty*—every young woman should read that book, every parent should read it, every boyfriend should read it. It should be mandatory reading for . . . well . . . everybody.

16 Song of Songs 8:12.

17 The best article I've ever read on the passage in Ephesians 5 is called *Balls and Chains,* and it's by Gordon Gano of the band Violent Femmes (*Details,* July 1993). I've also found the writings of Jean Kilbourne to be insightful, especially *Can't Buy Me Love: How Advertising Changes the Way We Think and Feel* and *Deadly Persuasion: Why Women and Girls Must Fight the Addictive Power of Advertising.*

18 I heard Erwin McManus several years ago give a talk on being grateful that was very profound. It's now out as a book called *Uprising.*

CHAPTER SEVEN **UNDER THE CHUPPAH**

1 Exodus 3.

2 For a brilliant and unabashedly hopeful look at how to end poverty, read Jeffrey Sach's *The End of Poverty.*

3 The four promises in Exodus 6 are represented in the Passover meal by the drinking of four cups, which raises the question, When Jesus was having a Passover meal with his disciples (Matt. 26), which cup did he raise? For more on the meal, the cups, and their significance for Jesus and his followers, study the materials called *Torah Club* by First Fruits of Zion (ffoz.org).

4 The cloud appears in 1 Kings 8:10 at the dedication of the temple.

5 Exodus 19:5.

6 Verse 8.

7 Verses 10–11.

8 Verses 14–15.

9 Hosea 1–2.

10 Malachi 2:14.

11 Numbers 15:38.

12 Song of Songs 1.

13 Exodus 22:16.

14 Deuteronomy 22:28–29.

15 William Webb's *Slaves, Women, and Homosexuals* is a systematic, detailed explanation of this truth about the Bible.

16 Gwyneth Paltrow on the breakup of Brad Pitt and Jennifer Aniston: "'It would have been a lot easier on Brad Pitt and Jennifer Aniston now if they had not talked to the press about each other and everything to begin with . . . I learned my lesson at 24.' Paltrow, now married to Coldplay frontman Chris Martin, values her privacy. 'Our marriage is between us,' she says. 'If we decide to continue being together or not, it's our business'" (*Vanity Fair,* August 29, 2005).

17 Every couple thinking about getting married should read Sheldon Vanauken's *A Severe Mercy.*

18 Malcolm Gladwell's book *Blink* deals extensively with thin slicing.

CHAPTER EIGHT **JOHNNY AND JUNE**

1 Cash *Unearthed* box set book, page 27.

2 Genesis 2.

3 Genesis 2:18.

4 Psalm 121:1-2.

5 Psalm 89:19.

6 Genesis 2:23.

7 Verse 24. The man leaves? This is unusual. Generally the weaker leaves the parents and goes to the stronger. But Adam leaves his parents. Gilbert Bilezikian offers wonderful commentary on this in his book *Beyond Sex Roles.*

8 "Male and female are called to be one body and soul" (*Talmud menachot* 93a).

9 Genesis 2:24.

10 Dr. Rufus from the University of Stellenbosch in South Africa did the research and gave me these numbers:

The English language: 100,000 to 200,000 words in the dictionary; 500,000 words total in the language; and together with technical words 1,000,000.

The Hebrew language: 7,000.

11 The word *echad* actually is quite complex, implying a unity with multiple parts. We speak of a team playing "as one," a group of people discussing something as being "of one mind." "One nation," which can be made up of thousands or even millions of people.

12 Deuteronomy 6:4.

13 Christians traditionally break the Ten Commandments into two categories: commandments that deal with our relationship to

God (the first four), and commandments that deal with our relationships with each other (the remaining six). Christians generally put the fifth commandment, honoring your parents, in the second category.

The ancient rabbis, however, don't divide it this way. They put honoring your parents in the first set, making the division five and five. They saw that in creating new life, parents play a godlike role in the world. Their having sex has the potential to bring another human being, another soul, into existence. This is something only God can do—the creation of life—and God has given this ability to the man and the woman.

A man and a woman had sex and gave the world Nelson Mandela.

A man and woman had sex and gave us Mother Teresa and Martin Luther King Jr. and Albert Einstein.

And a man and woman had sex and gave us Adolf Hitler and Joseph Stalin and Pol Pot and thousands and millions of others who have affected the course of human history.

Sex is loaded with potential. With possibility. In some deeply mysterious way, the encounter between a man and a woman is loaded with the weight of the world. Who knows what this act of sex could create? Who knows *who* it could create?

Sex carries within it the power of life itself. It is not an isolated act with no consequences. There is always the possibility that human history will be significantly altered by what this man and this woman are about to do.

Something given by the creator of the universe. Something divine.

It isn't just that they are "making love." It's that they may end up making something else.

Somebody else.

14 Genesis 2:25.

15 Psalms about heart (14:1) and spirit (77:6) and flesh (84:2).

16 Song of Songs 2:7.

17 From "Double the Pleasure: Treating His Sexual Woes Also Boosts Her Satisfaction," by Brian Alexander (msnbc.com, November 10, 2005):

When Dr. Irwin Goldstein, a well-known expert in sexual medicine, presented recent research findings to a scientific meeting, he said: "It is rare for me to stand in front of an audience and say, 'This is a manuscript that has changed my life.' But this one has done that."

At first glance the study, printed in the Journal of Sexual Medicine (edited by Goldstein), seems like the most obvious thing in the world. When you hear the results, you say to yourself, "Well, duh!"

The results showed that female sexual partners in committed relationships with men who were treated with an impotence drug (in this case Levitra, made by Bayer, which also sponsored the study) had better sex. That's the "duh" part. But get this: the women's bodies reacted as if they were receiving the drug, as if they were the ones being treated. So a drug they didn't even take affected their bodies.

"Her physiology is linked to him," Goldstein says. "Men share problems with women, and the solutions. . . . I can change someone's physiology without treating them. It's the wildest thing!"

There's a concept in the world of physics called "entanglement." It refers to the weird fact that subatomic particles have "partners"—other subatomic particles—with which they can be entangled, sometimes over great distances. If a physicist tinkers with one particle, the change affects the other particle. Strange but true.

I find Goldstein's study a strong indicator that humans can be entangled, that the romantic ideal extolled by poets and Dr. Phil exists in real life. We really change when we fall in love. We become a unit, at least sexually. "There are no other physiologic abilities of men and women that are shared, and that is what is so fascinating about these data," Goldstein says.

18 Have you observed people who have to have a radio on, the television on, or their iPod nearby? Are you one of those people?

One of the reasons some have to always have noise and external stimulus is because they are terrified of the silence. The stillness. The present. If you stop and rest in the quiet, you will have to listen to what is going on inside of you. And this can be frightening.

Imagine a person who never listens to their own soul, who never sits in the silence with themselves, who is never naked with themselves. Imagine this person trying to become *echad* with another. How can a person mingle with another soul when they are out of touch with their own?

Ask yourself the following questions and write down whatever comes to mind. Get rid of your edit button. No one's going to read this. You'll throw it away afterward. Maybe.

But seriously, try this. Write out your answers to these questions:

What is frustrating me right now?

What am I angry about?

No, don't go to the next one, go back. Listen. Reflect. Be honest. Give yourself time. The book will be here when you get back.

What am I scared of?

What am I dreading?

What am I anxious about?

What concerns me?

What is stressing me right now, the smallest thing that I don't want to write down because it seems so dumb but it actually is stressing me?

What am I looking forward to?

Today, tomorrow, this year?

It's amazing how many people do this exercise and discover that there are all sorts of things right below the surface that they weren't aware of. It can be jarring to learn about yourself. To learn that all sorts of things are brewing on the inside that we've missed.

Now, if you're with someone, if you've given yourself to another, how do you feel about sharing your list?

19 Watch the final scene in *Pride and Prejudice* (2005) when

Elizabeth and Mr. Darcy meet in the field in the morning. What do they do? Or more precisely, what don't they do? Why did the director close with that scene?

CHAPTER NINE **WHOOPEE FOREVER**

1 Matthew 19:12.

2 Luke 20:34–36.

3 Verse 6.

4 1 Corinthians 7:7–9.

5 Verses 25–28.

6 Verses 28, 32–34, 39–40. An odd line, isn't it? Someone who wrote a good portion of the New Testament saying that he thinks that he too has the "Spirit of God."

7 Revelation 21:1–2. John actually got the "new heaven, new earth" part from the prophet Isaiah (chaps. 65–66).

8 Verse 22:3.

9 Verse 23.

10 Verse 27.

11 22:2.

12 Verse 3.

13 21:5.

14 If you are having any sort of "Woah!" moment, I suggest reading *The Divine Romance* by Gene Edwards.

15 See Ray Vander Laan and Judith Markham's *Echoes of His Presence.*

16 Matthew 25:1–13.